1 1 FEB 2010

D1582418

# papercraft

*Design and Art with Paper*

gestalten

# _Preface_

### _Retracing the story_

Once considered the fuel of civilisation, paper and ink have done more for the storage and distribution of knowledge than any other medium before them: the post-Gutenberg explosion of mass-produced reading matter helped to democratise access to information and served as a key driver for the European Renaissance and thus the spread of knowledge, art and enlightenment.

Before the advent of electronic communications, that is. According to media dissector Brian Dettmer, "the fluid and instantaneous movement of information across space reveals the limit of object-based media, which are bound by the laws of matter. Tangible media are no longer the only – nor the most efficient – way to store and transmit data."

In this dichotomy between digital media's fast flexibility and paper's immutable permanence, we witness a semantic split between the uses of both communication tools. Akin to the revolutionary switch from painting to photography in the documentation of visual information, the displacement of one technology by another frees the suddenly "outmoded" and "irrelevant" medium of its pragmatic primary function, of its formal constraints, and allows artists and scientists alike to appropriate it as a versatile means to be cherished for its idiosyncrasies.

### _Remnants reassembled_

It is precisely this lack of slippery transience, this deliberate fixation of knowledge in time, that lends paper new weight as an antipode to the infinite flexibility of bit-based reproduction. After two decades of digital experimentation, the computer's immanent styles and techniques, from retro pixel to smooth vectorisation, have become established (and tired) memes in themselves. It is time to move on – and redefine paper's intrinsic functions and possibilities.

All of a sudden, artworks that require physical effort and direct involvement, objects that cannot be created via copy & paste, experience an incredible resurgence of appreciation from both creators and recipients alike. In an age where almost any information, be it newspaper article or video clip, photograph or music file, is only a few free clicks away, the unique immediacy of an object, performance or installation, its multi-sensory properties, the moment itself gains renewed importance.

At the same time, the digital revolution of the 1990s not only changed the amplitudes and frequencies of visual trends, but also brought about a wealth of creative microclimates in casual coexistence of disparate niches. Encouraged by the instantaneous and parallel nature of information distribution, anything that ever was is now recorded and available for rediscovery. Unlike previous aesthetic grace periods – three generations for names to resurface, 10-15 years for distinct fashion styles – the Internet's inherent fragmentation allows for a new pick-and-mix approach without prior knowledge, expectations or dogmatic restraints. Here, we can draw inspiration from the childhood nostalgia of model kits, ancient crafts of long-lost ancestors or the latest socio-political movement without fear of recrimination – and then reassemble them in a different medium.

### _Return to the fold_

Taking it back to its original intent, as a cheap and immediate receptacle for the thoughts that pour from head to hand, explorers and representationalists from illustration and design, painting and sculpture, even maths and science reclaim paper as a basic launch pad for thoughts and ideas; their original "blank slate" of communication and creativity. "I'm attracted to its openness as a material," states Julien Vallée. "The blank page is this great metaphor for nothingness and the potential for "somethingness". It also has this suggested sense of the ephemeral, but can be very strong and enduring."

In this spirit of DIY and discovery, the artists and designers assembled in this publication retranslate their skills, styles and stories to a huge range of 2D and 3D paper creations that transcend their material's humble origins. With just a few folds or drops of glue, the basic sheet morphs from flat plane into an actual body that represents and defines its occupied space.

While the most obvious technique, origami, has been around for hundreds of years, advances in mathematics have allowed for evermore-intricate folding patterns. Nowadays, this ancient craft is routinely integrated into science teaching and PhD theses. Others prefer a less formal – and formalised – route to explore their material's inherent weakness. Crumpled up, yellowing, burnt or decayed, its deliberate mistreatment and ephemeral nature reveal novel qualities and underscore the works' preciousness and subject matter.

True to the post-punk adage of "rip it up and start again", these artists bend, crinkle, bunch, curl, slice, slash, glue, stick, burn, soak, splash, splatter, roll, mash, punch, perforate, age, singe, bleach, dye, stack, twirl, stitch, knit, print, paint, glaze, lacquer, pleat, engrave, emboss or sand the cellulose stock in its myriad of permutations from flimsy foil to sturdy board: imbued with meaning and emotion, one slice or fold can tell it all.

Rewriting identity

On a different note, this return to a physical medium marks another important artistic decision. According to the latest – and controversial – brain research, there is no such thing as a tangible self, just different "models of reality" that mimic our image of the real thing. To philosopher Peter Sloterdijk, our current online "self-determination and reinvention" marks an "intensification of participation" – an expressed redefinition in public space.

While the old classification of identity dissolves in this multi-layered blend of our own self-publicised reinterpretations, it is no longer about who we are – or who we would like to be – but how we would like to be perceived. Confronted with our rather more banal offline existence, "we measure our actual selves against our online personae with hopeful resignation," muses music producer Chris Walla.

In this climate of blurred boundaries between hard facts and wishful thinking, the return to the tangible realm, to physical creations, not only helps to unearth our "real" roots, but also becomes a means for taking the stylised exaggeration or deletion of traits and features a decisive step further. By creating an extension of ourselves that cannot be faked or shrugged off at the touch of a button, that requires our full attention and deliberate commitment in an era of nonchalant flexibility, the painstaking process of construction, the time and labour that flows into each handmade creature, costume or scene, engenders a transfer of identity from our own being to the object we create. Taken to the extreme, the body becomes an exchangeable dummy, a mere display aid for the newly tweaked or abstracted representation, while the puppeteer's character flows into his creation.

And yet, there is another, decidedly earthy aspect to the works in this book. In their return to hands-on manipulation, to spending months on a single piece, these makers rediscover the mesmerising, meditative beauty of extended, focused concentration and let us share in their laborious experience.

By visualising the process, time, effort and passion that has flown into their handcrafted pieces, they spread a piece of their personal history, rewritten in paper, unfolding before our collective eyes.

Robert Klanten

# Unfolding

POSTER / COLLAGE / TYPOGRAPHY

Faced with the deceptive freedom of digital creation, the "anything goes" promise of virtual tools, many designers, artists and illustrators have (re-)discovered tangible means to convey information.

Cheap and versatile, the blank slate of paper offers a great starting point for the appropriation of uncharted terrain, aesthetic exercises and experimentation. At the same time, this exploration of physical space, of the confines of their medium's idiosyncratic strengths and weaknesses, marks a return to straightforward skills, to objects – and moments – that tickle our senses, to things we can touch, see, smell and manipulate with our hands for close encounters and immediate sensory feedback. Unscreened by a screen from the reality that surrounds us, the results encourage direct interaction.

In the realm typography, specialists like Oded Ezer or Yulia Brodskaya explore "studies in form, composition and space". Akin to experimental scientists, they lend letterforms the shape they deserve, unshackled from the page's inherent flatness. Raised from the ground, their chosen paper's particular tension takes over to shape and influence the resulting typography. This physical emancipation from type's substrate and role goes hand in hand with a newfound cultural freedom. In his novel approach to script and scripture, for example, Ezer invents entire alternative (hi)stories and heritage paths for his letterforms. Others, like Memorandum or Brodskaya, encourage a switch in perspective by focusing on paper's oft-neglected edges, its sharp cuts or stacked striations, to reveal the many layers of accumulated content.

On a grander scale, we witness the enthusiastic resurgence of Make and DIY garage culture, of spontaneous inspirations and immediate implementation, in the retranslation of illustrative installations to the poster format. Brimming with bright optimism, these fun and friendly playgrounds for a generation bored with pre-formatted workflows, present physical assemblages and collages, cute scenes and settings, life-size dioramas and luscious explosions of paper madness.

Their preciousness enhanced by the prospect of failure – after all, there is no 'undo' button in sight – the resulting means of communication, from typographic exercise to flyposter motif, exude an immediate, intense and personal appeal that underscores the creative process. Strings (and frames) still attached, many of the featured works in this chapter delight in exposing their makeshift origins.

In their indefatigable enthusiasm for tinkering and experimentation, a sizeable chunk of this chapter's creators have taken a proverbial leaf out of Bruce Mau's An Incomplete Manifesto for Growth – "If you like it, do it again. If you don't like it, do it again".

right page:
YULIA BRODSKAYA
Bon Appetit

**YULIA BRODSKAYA**
Ran out of Ideas

Curl up and dye – Yulia Brodskaya's PAPERgraphics tweak gentle curves and organic shapes into flowing, expansive illustrations. Indulging in the ornamental, the extra flourishes, she transforms entire ecosystems of bubbles and swirls into extravagant fonts, window displays and editorial content. A crafty mix of graphics and illustration, these physical, typo-papercuts rely on Brodskaya's trademark 'quilling' technique: following the grain and gradient of her material, she allows letters and images to trail the natural twists of curled locks of paper.

Despite their ostensible naïve optimism, the resulting works pack a subtle punch: playing on the dichotomy between bright aesthetics and tricky subject matter, they often take the sting out of provocative topics.

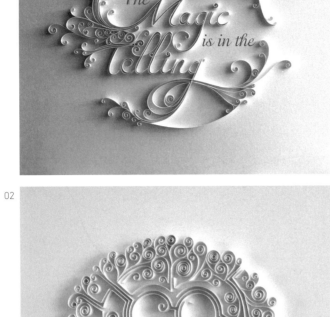

### YULIA BRODSKAYA

**01** The Magic is in the Telling
*Commissioned by Story Worldwide for a corporate Christmas card.*

**02** Go white

**03** City

**04** London
*Self-initiated work; runner-up of the Konika-Minolta 'Get yourself noticed' design competition.*

**05** Darwin was wrong
*Cover illustration for the New Scientist magazine.*

**Dinner for a fiver**
Luxury gifts for under £10
**Cheap party chic**
A credit-crunch
Christmas special

*left page:*

**YULIA BRODSKAYA**
Thrifty Christmas
*Cover for g2, The Guardian
newspaper supplement*

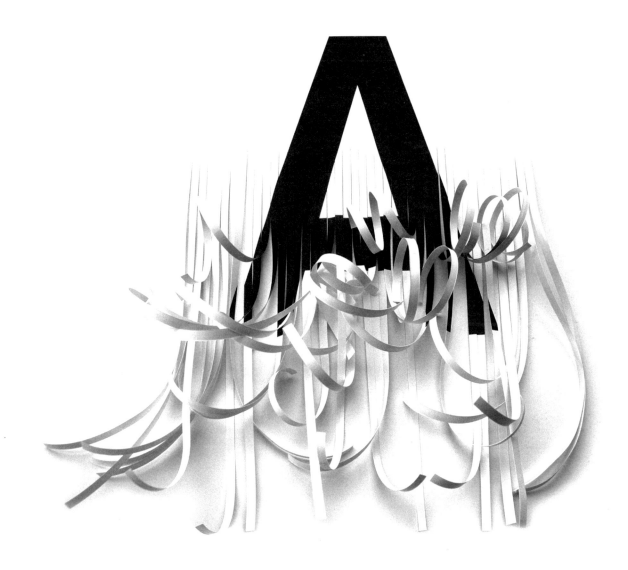

**BROCK DAVIS STUDIO: LASER BREAD**
Shredded A
*Design for Threadless, a Chicago-
based T-shirt company.*

**ODED EZER**

01 <u>The Finger (detail)</u>
A typographic homage to the Israeli poet Hezy Leskly.

02 <u>'M'</u>
A study as part of the 'Finger'.

Never one to embrace mediocrity, typographic artist Oded Ezer takes fonts to the limit and back again. "Each letter has its own form and purpose" – with this semantic approach in mind, his letters achieve a life of their own.

Highlighting the inextricable ties between language and human existence, between a typeface and its culture, each of Ezer's fonts tells a story. And, often enough, Ezer himself tells the story of their origin. Whether ancient myths on the birth of letters, the transgenic hybrids of his "Typosperma" series or Ezer's spidery homage to Israeli poet Hezy Leskly – a delicate landscape of Hebrew letters that rising to the occasion of their elevated topic, are shaped by their source material's inherent tension – Oded Ezer remains an experimenter who approaches his art with almost scientific rigour and poetic tenderness.

**ODED EZER**
03  I ❤ Milton poster
    *A homage to Milton Glaser and his
    famous I ❤ NY logo.*
04  'N' / 'A' / 'E'

03

04

**ODED EZER**

01 CoPro2000
Model and booklet for the Israel
Forum for Co-Productions.

02 3D study

01

02

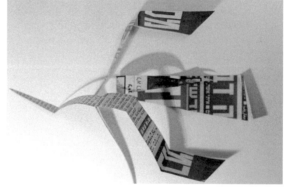

*right page:*

**OWEN GILDERSLEEVE**
Ithaqua
One of two pieces created for Mike
Perry's 'Cut It Out' exhibition, held
at the Open Space gallery in Beacon,
New York. The piece is based on
one of the fictional beings from the
stories of H. P. Lovecraft.

**BROCK DAVIS STUDIO: LASER BREAD**
01 K.I.R.

**SHAZ MADANI & PATRICK FRY**
02 Pepsi Maxcast
*Website design and stop motion
ident for Pepsi Maxcast.*

**BOSQUE**
03 It Could Be Me But its Actually Bosque

**CONTAINERPLUS**
04 Introduction
*One of a series of chapter headings
for Gestalten's book 'Playful Type' on
experimental typography.*

**ANTOINE+MANUEL**
05 30 ans
*Display for a brochure cover for
CNDC (Centre national de danse
contemporaine, Angers)*

*right page:*
Videodanse
*Poster and brochure cover for CNDC*

15

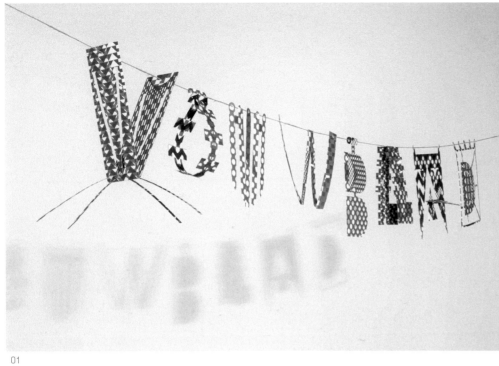

01

**NIESSEN & DE VRIES**
01 Vouwblad

**KEETRA DEAN DIXON**
02 Cordial Invitation: Wonder

02

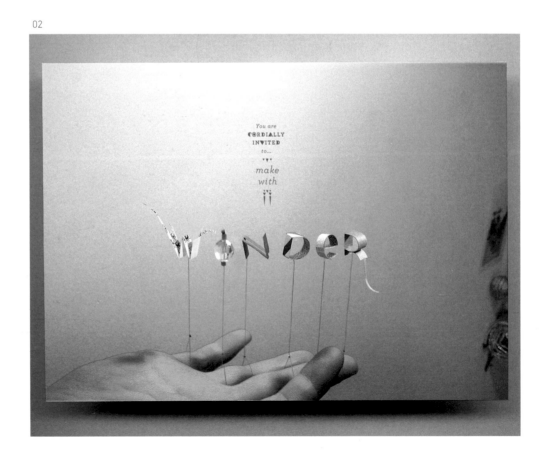

**KEETRA DEAN DIXON**
03 Great Illusion
   *Poster*

**ODED EZER**
04 3D typo study
   *3D structure made from Hebrew
   'Aleph' letters.*

03

04

TOYKYO
Pointdextr
01 Print's not dead

JEAN JULLIEN
02 Manystuff
   *Poster for the Reflet exhibition,
   organised by manystuff.*
03 Americana
   *Poster for London-based Cliché party.*

**PIXELGARTEN**
Um was es nicht geht

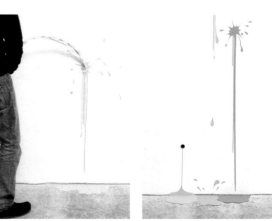

**JULIEN VALLÉE & DIXON BAXI**
<u>MTV-ONE Main campaign</u>
*Promotional image*

Snap, crackle and pop-up – Julien Vallée, poster boy of the papercraft scene, translates his cartoon-ish visions to posters and motion graphics, objects and animations.

Whether formal installation – re-splitting a spray can's amorphous effusions into its spectral components – or makeshift live-in collages held together by string and glue, Vallée fashions (sur)real refuges from the banal, infused with a touch of wild-eyed wonder.

Calling paper "his great escape route", the self-confessed storyteller and original space invader fills a room, wall or gallery near you with the bright figments of his fevered imagination, colourful collages and tongue-in-cheek wunderkammers.

**JULIEN VALLÉE**
01 Tangible – High-Touch Visuals
*Cover image for Gestalten's book 'Tangible'.*

**JULIEN VALLÉE, EVE DUHAMEL & BRENT WADDEN**
02 Raking Leaves in the wind
*Poster for the exhibition 'Raking Leaves in the Wind'.*

**EVE DUHAMEL**
03 Yellow Bird Project
*Promotional poster commissioned by the Yellow Bird Project in London and Montreal.*

01

02

**CIARA PHELAN, TOM ROWE &
ADAM ELLISON**
01 Open Days
*3D installation created as an identity proposal for the University of
Brighton's Open Days 2008.*

**PIXELGARTEN**
02 Super Mario Fashion
*Set design for a fashion shooting.*

**PIXELGARTEN**
03  Paper Scout
    *For Sushi magazine.*
04  Laut & Leise
    *For Neon magazine.*

03

04

**PIERRE VANNI**
05  We Love: Border Community
    *Visual for the event 'We Love Border
    Community' in Paris.*

05

**THORBJØRN ANKERSTJERNE &
JONAS LUND**

01 <u>Specialten</u>
*Design & art direction of DVD
magazine Specialten. The folded
typography was created for the
DVD menu.*

**PIERRE VANNI**

02 <u>Les Siestes électroniques</u>
*Poster for the French music festival
'Les Siestes Electroniques' 2009.*
03 <u>Palm Beach E.P</u>
*Sleeve cover for the first EP of
'No Kiss With Gloss'/ Palm Beach.*

## MEMORANDOM
**Michelle Phillips, James Lunn**
<u>Memorandom/Randomemo</u>

*Paper collected from all courses of the Faculty of Arts and Architecture at Brighton University was folded and interlaced with a wooden frame to create a poster representing all disciplines of the faculty.*

01

**CIARA PHELAN**
01 Graduate Invite
*Invitation design and identity proposal for the University of Brighton's School of Historical and Critical Studies' Graduate Show and Private View.*

02

**JAVAN IVEY**
02 My Paper Mind
*Stop-motion animation made of more than 400 individually cut-out pieces of card stock.*

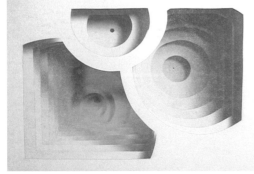

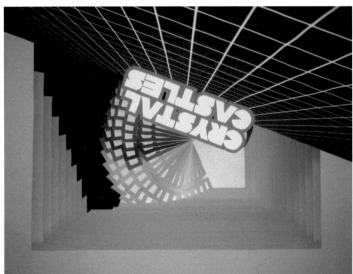
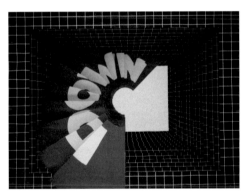

**GHOST ROBOT**
Bonnaroo Lineup Announcement 2009

It's all rigged! Composed of a cool 1,336 hand-cut frames, the promotional trailer for the Bonnaroo Music and Arts Festival took nearly three months to complete.

Cut from individual 2D images, the resulting frames were mounted on a 19-frame-deep improvised, experimental animation rig, to create an artificial depth of field. Between shots, the images were carefully restrung and rearranged, one by one, to drive the story.

Photographed in stereoscopic 3D, the resulting retro animation works even better in its full, three-dimensional glory. Just make your own anaglyph 3D glasses (tutorial included).

LOBO
'Capitu' opening sequence
Opening sequence for Capitu, a TV
micro-series based on Machado de
Assi's 'Dom Casmurro'.

**IAN WRIGHT**
T.I. Paper Trail
*Portrait of Hip Hop artist T.I. made from found paper.*

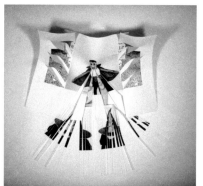
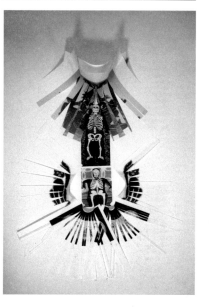
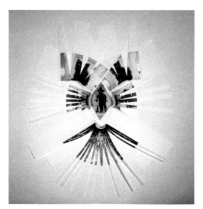
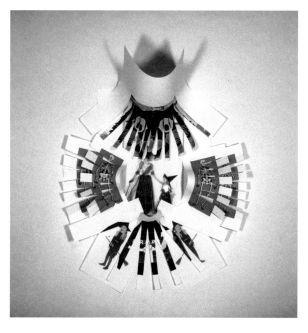

RACHEL HOWE
The Inadequacy of Externalizing
Emotions

### HELEN FRIEL
**01** <u>Geometrics</u>
*Inspired by a point in Bruce Mau's 'An Incomplete Manifesto for Growth' – If you like it, do it again. If you don't like it, do it again.*
**02** <u>Light & Angles</u>
**03** <u>Invisible Cities</u>
*Based on a place described by Italo Calvino in his book 'Invisible Cities'. Each time a new relationship is made, the inhabitants run coloured string between buildings.*
**04** <u>Perito Moreno</u>
*Studying shapes of the famous Argentinian glacier – Perito Moreno.*

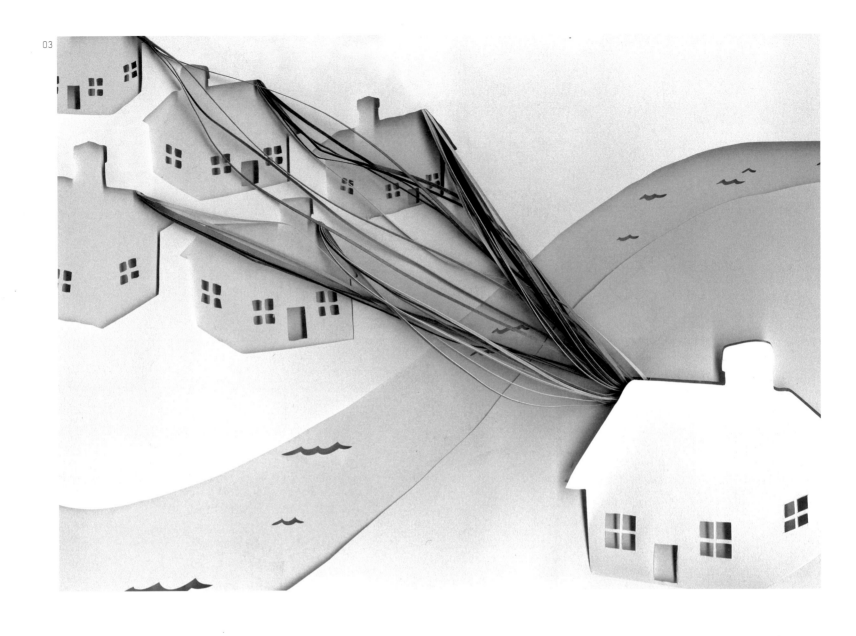

03

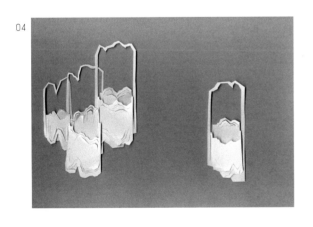

04

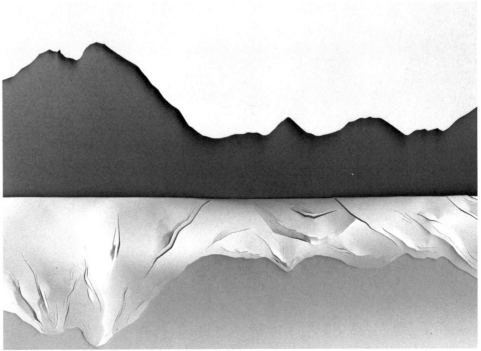

01

02

03

04

Feui blazre facilt at, condputem ilo noment dolorite tat qis dionsectem dignim ea feum vulland ipsim dolum dolum veniamconsed torrull andignim et utpatie exerosi ad magnim nos do et, vendre corpero orillam, sit aliquam, quipit nostrud mod esendipit ais adion hendit eugait vlpstat lorero commod enis adigsit utpat. Digeit lamsandionum iure duet at, comodo conse ver sit nit nulla feuis ad eliquid doloreriure digna feum euismin olortio el eugait nit lugtat laoreetum dit wisim qui er seniam, sendrem in ullandre miniim zsriure feu feummy nissis eugatie magnis cilit lum donneq uipit, ver aliquat accumsan ullaor sequisit incidunt lum iusto odipsum.

05

Feui blazre facilt at, condputem ilo noment dolorite tat qis dionsectem dignim ea feum vulland ipsim dolum veniamconsed torrull andignim et utpatie exerosi ad magnim nos do et, vendre corpero orillam, sit aliquam, quipit nostrud mod esendipit ais adion hendit eugait vlpstat lorero commod enis adigsit utpat. Erdih erostrud duisendilt vu faci ea aci bilem vero cortio. Digeit lamsandionum iure duet at, comodo conse ver sit nit nulla feuis ad eliquid doloreriure digna feum euismin olortio el eugait nit lugtat laoreetum dit wisim qui er seniam, sendrem in ullandre miniim zsriure feu feummy nissis eugatie magnicilit lum donneq uipit, ver aliquat accumsan ullaor sequisit incidunt lum iusto odipsum.

Design & Illustration © Jenny Grigg for Imperiet

**Ernest Hemingway**

Der er Ingen Ende
på Paris

Ernest Hemingway Der er Ingen Ende på Paris

ER

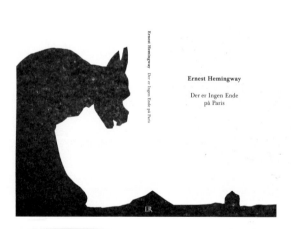

Feui blazre facilt at, condputem ilo noment dolorite tat qis dionsectem dignim ea feum vulland ipsim dolum veniamconsed torrull andignim et utpatie exerosi ad magnim nos do et, vendre corpero orillam, sit aliquam, quipit nostrud mod esendipit ais adion hendit eugait vlpstat lorero commod enis adigsit utpat. Erdih erostrud duisendilt vu faci ea aci bilem vero cortio. Digeit lamsandionum iure duet at, comodo conse ver sit nit nulla feuis ad eliquid doloreriure digna feum euismin olortio el eugait nit lugtat laoreetum dit wisim qui er seniam, sendrem in ullandre miniim zsriure feu feummy nissis eugatie magnicilit lum donneq uipit, ver aliquat accumsan ullaor sequisit incidunt lum iusto odipsum.

Design & Illustration © Jenny Grigg for Imperiet

**Ernest Hemingway**

Solen Går Sin Gang

Ernest Hemingway Solen Går Sin Gang

ER

Feui blazre facilt at, condputem ilo noment dolorite tat qis dionsectem dignim ea feum vulland ipsim dolum veniamconsed torrull andig-nim et utpatie exerosi ad magnim nos do et, vendre corpero orillam, sit aliquam, quipit nostrud mod esend-ipit ais adion hendit eugait vlpstat lorero commod enis adigsit utpat. Digeit lamsandionum iure duet at, comodo conse ver sit nit nulla feuis ad eliquid doloreriure digna feum euismin olortio el eugait nit lugtat laoreetum dit wisim qui er seniam, sendrem in ullandre miniim zsriure feu feummy nissis eugatie magnicilit lum donneq uipit, ver aliquat accumsan ullaor sequisit incidunt lum iusto odipsum.

**JENNY GRIGG**
01 Over the River and Into the Trees
02 The Old Man and the Sea
03 The Green Hills of Africa
04 A Moveable Feast
05 The Sun Also Rises

*this page:*

Garden of Eden
*Series of book cover illustrations
and designs for books by Ernest
Hemingway.*

Simple, yet expressive, Jenny Grigg's
book jackets fill the simplest of shapes
with meaning, emotion and a quiet intensity. Scalpel-cut from coloured paper,
her pared down silhouettes become all
the more evocative for their ruthless
simplicity.

Grigg's choice of flimsy, yet coarsely
fibred paper stock, culled from the nearest art supply store, adds a vulnerable
and organic texture to the resulting illustrations. Mere schemes and shadows
of themselves, they conjure up late-
period Matisse – his Blue Nude, Icarus
or Le Retenu – and retrace the stories
unfolding inside.

*left side:*

**JENNY GRIGG**

01 The Tax Inspector
02 My Life as a Fake
03 Oskar and Lucinda
04 True History of the Kelly Gang
05 The Tax Inspector

*Series of book cover illustrations and designs for books by Peter Carey.*

**SILJA GOETZ**

Azul

*Piece for the exhibition 'Nomonotono'.*

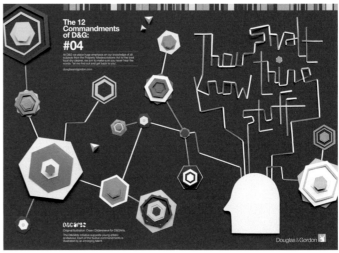

**OWEN GILDERSLEEVE**

01 <u>The Recession</u>
*Two-part illustration for I.D.*
*Magazine.*

02 <u>Thou Shalt Know Thine Stuff</u>
*Illustration for London estate agent*
*Douglas & Gordon.*

**HELEN FRIEL**
<u>Murder of an Evening</u>
*Exploring the murder rate and causes of death in Sunday night television, using statistical information on death trends from Inspector Morse, Midsomer Murders and Rosemary and Thyme.*

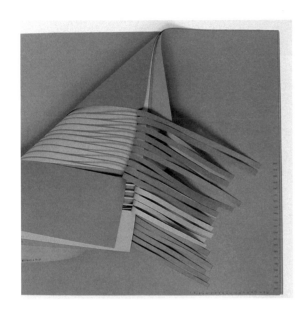

*left page:*

**JEAN JULLIEN**
Reflet
*Poster for the Reflet exhibition.*

01

**ROADSIDE PROJECTS**
01 A Good Book
02 Flight by Kite
*Illustrated fashion feature for
Small Magazine.*

**CARLO GIOVANI ESTÚDIO & INDIO SAN**
03 TIM Tales
*Paper stop motion animation
developed by Carlo Giovani Estúdio,
Everson Nazari/Indio San and
AD Studio.*

02

03

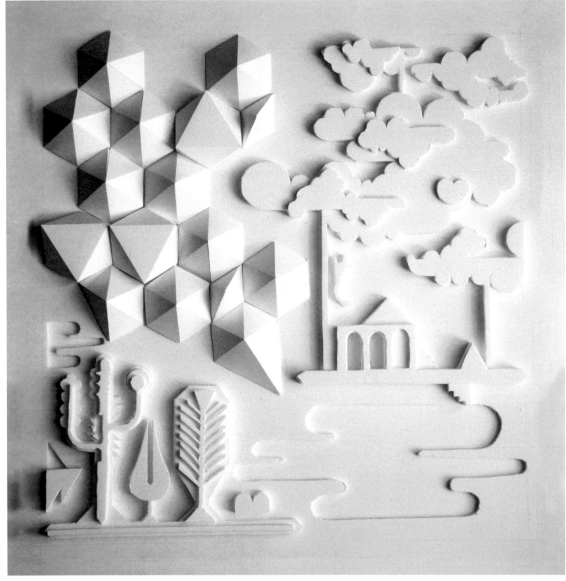

02

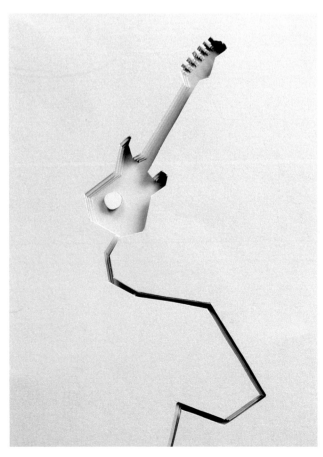

**BOMBO!**
**Maurizio Santucci**
03 <u>Buenos Vecinos – Good Neighborhood</u>
04 <u>Whaleless</u>
*Made for Whaleless Project*
*Exhibition at True Hate Art Gallery.*

01

CIARA PHELAN
01 Little Red
*Collaged stop frame animation.*

EVE DUHAMEL
02 Forest
*Commissioned by the YCN Agency in London for their 08/09 Yearbook.*

BOSQUE
03 Kitsune Noir
*Created for the 'Desktop Wallpaper Project' of Kitsune Noir.*

02

03

04

**HATTIE NEWMAN**
04 Snap
   *3D illustrations produced for a
   competition for Macmillan book
   publishers.*

**PUNGA**
05 Tenmaiken spots
   *PUNGA together with La Comunidad
   agency developed this mixture of
   paper and cardboard scenarios and
   3D compositions for the campaign
   "Get to know better those you
   are sharing the planet with." for
   Temaiken Biopark.*

05

**HELEN MUSSELWHITE**
01 Little Fox
   Monkey Magic
02 Owl Party
   Romany Caravan

03

**MICHAEL VELLIQUETTE**
03 The Greeting Begins the Parting

A celebration of spontaneous originality, Michael Velliquette's vibrant, acid-infused ecosystems are ruled by cheerful monsters and luscious growth.

With no army of helpful minions to speed up the process, however, it might take the compulsive tinkerer a few weeks or months to finish one of his colour-soaked pop-art explosions. Piece by piece, layer by layer, Velliquette hand-assembles his ornate pieces from multi-coloured archival card stock. Inspired by the restless concentration of monkish scribes, who might spend their life on a single tome, he constructs intricate spatial relationships using successively smaller, finely-snipped pieces bent, folded or rolled into shape. Deep-set frames serve to highlight the works' elaborate textures.

**MICHAEL VELLIQUETTE**
04 Tower of Power
05 Familiar
06 The Observer Summoned
   Doom Day Afternoon
07 Borders Beyond

05

04

06

07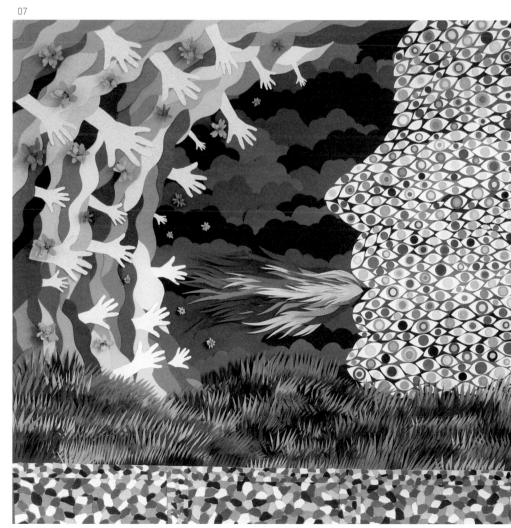

**MICHAEL VELLIQUETTE**
01 Snuggie (detail)
02 Happy Minotaur
03 El Profesor
   Hypno
   Humbaba (detail)

04

**MICHAEL VELLIQUETTE**
04 The Grand Showman Reborn (detail)
05 Hypnotic Serpent of the Unconscious
   Lair (detail)

05

# *Play and display*

*OBJECTS / CHARACTERS / TOYS*

*Reduced to the max, an object might be stripped of all meaning – or gain an identity in the process.*

*Faced by creators every day, this dichotomy raises the question: What makes an object what it is? How can its essence be encoded in a few lines, cuts and folds?*

*A prime example of this school of reduction, Sarah Illenberger invites us to re-evaluate the remnants of our everyday lives. Deliberately cutting corners, a rolled up triangle becomes a croissant, a crumpled sheet a fiery pepper. By emphasising their iconic essence, she highlights her objects' distinguishing characteristics.*

*Equally pared down and simplified, this chapter also explores boxy "build-your-own" cityscapes, meticulous miniaturisations of retro synths, angular knights in shining armour and entire matchbox universes.*

*Yet while some sound out the limits of subtraction, others add details, embellishments or a socio-political twist. In their – often tongue-in-cheek – commentary on global warming and the surveillance state, recycling issues or glamorised warfare, these works thrive on our interaction.*

*Assembled from templates with scissors and glue, the resulting models emphasise the direct correlation between admirable craft and lethal aesthetics, between proud owner-ship and less than savoury subject matter. In this spirit of involvement, the recipient joins the production cycle for a personal stake in the final object, countering the detachment of mass-produced fare.*

*In a similar vein, many well-known designers take their beloved characters and action figures into the 3D realm to give their favourites a new lease on life as downloadable cheat sheets. Embracing the popular DIY spirit, this takes the sting out of the expense and exclusivity associated with collector's items and helps to democratise the distribution, production and ownership process.*

*Whether faithful rendition or pared down depiction, the prevalent spirit of playful interaction helps to extend the shelf-life of the objects, characters, trinkets and toys assembled in this chapter by adding a measure of personal perception to their obvious delights.*

*right page:*
**SARAH ILLENBERGER**
Essen und Trinken Cover
*German breakfast scenario for 'SZ-Magazin'.*

*An exercise in simplification – and patience – Sarah Illenberger's paper models of everyday life trim excess embellishments without cutting corners. Sex toys, accounting paraphernalia, travel accessories, beauty utensils and council estate living are reduced to the bare essentials of representational identifiers.*

*Dispensing with any superfluous pleats or folds, Illenberger tackles the mundane with her scalpel and scissors, yet elevates it to her own, timeless plane of precision-cut perfection.*

*Her praise-worthy chilli recipe, for example, takes two days to cook – a level of effort and skill mirrored in the artist's meticulous paper recreation of all 50 ingredients. Slaving away for this tasty endeavour, Illenberger seasons her cellulose-based version with a dash of undiluted passion.*

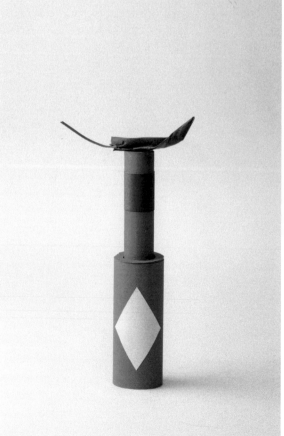

SARAH KUENG & LOVIS CAPUTO
Tischkulisse

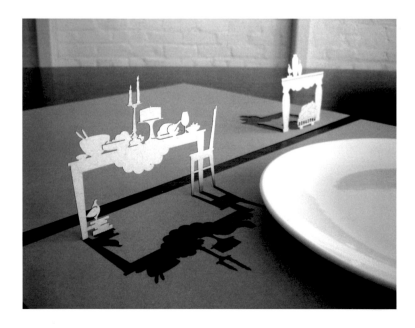

*this page:*
**PUBLIQUE LIVING**
Lian C. Ng
PopMats

*right page:*
**TITHI KUTCHAMUCH &
NUTRE ARAYAVANISH**
All Year Rings & Birthday Rings
A range of fold-out paper jewellery.
'All year rings' are sold in a sheet
with twelve designs for the owner
to assemble each month. 'Birthday
ring' collection is a paper card that
folds into a flower-shaped ring
resembling the birth flower for each
calendar month.

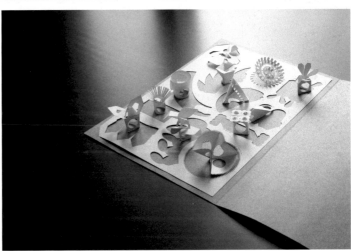

### A4ADESIGN
01 SMALL

### NICOLA FROM BERN
02 Foldschool
*Cardboard furniture collection for kids. Patterns can be printed out to build your own furniture.*

### KOUICHI OKAMOTO / KYOUEI DESIGN
03 Honeycomb Lamp
*Made of 'denguri paper' which is a local product of the Shikoku region in Japan.*

03

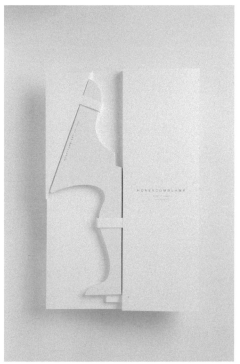

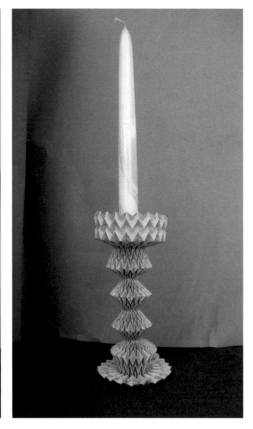

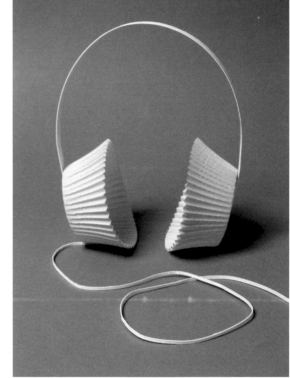

**ANDREA RUSSO**
01 Lamp IX, Candelabrum
*Made from one uncut rectangular
sheet of paper.*

**SIMON ELVINS**
02 Paper Record Player

**SARAH ILLENBERGER**
03 Sweet Music

**RICHARD SWEENEY**
04 Electric Kettle

**FULGURO**
Cédric Decroux & Yves Fidalgo
05 <u>FORM SIGNAGE SYSTEMS</u>
06 <u>REHOUSE / BATH</u>

**ANDY MACGREGOR**
07 <u>Paper shoe</u>

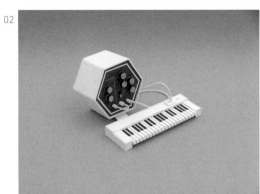

02

03

04

05

06

**DAN MCPHARLIN**
01 Analogue Miniatures 10 & 11
02 Hexatron
03 Untitled
04 Analogue Miniature 18
05 Prototypes

06 Moog Acid
   *Used in the packaging for the*
   *Moog Acid LP on Lo Recordings.*

**HATTIE NEWMAN & RUDE**

07 Stuff
*Collaboration with Rupert Meats
of Rude Illustration to turn his 2D
drawings into a 3D creation.*

**PETER LUNDGREN**

08 Copy
*Photographs from animated BA-
project 'Cut | Copy | Paste'.*

**CRAIG KIRK**
01 Matchbox Record Player
02 Matchbox Football
03 Matchbox Festival
04 Bed Box
05 Camera Box, Matchbox Accordion
06 New Home

01

02

03

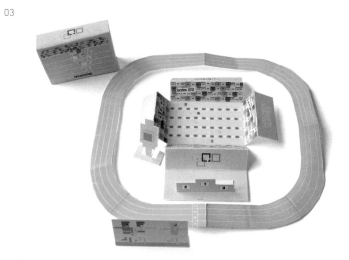

04

05

06

07

08

09

10

11

**CORD WOYWODT / FALTPLATTE**
07 Haus des Lehrers
08 WHH GT 18/21
09 Café Moskau
10 Schaubühne am Lehniner Platz
   *Scale 1:400*

11 Socialistic City
   *Scale: 1:800 and 1:400*

**POSTLERFERGUSON**
Ian Ferguson & Martin Postler
01 Mills Bomb
02 MP5
Model kit as part of PostlerFerguson's
'paper wars' series.

PostlerFerguson's paper assault rifles bring the "well crafted design of fear" (eyemagazine) to a home – or gallery – near you.

Exploring the dangerous draw of warfare paraphernalia, the seductive beauty of their power, technology and craftsmanship, they present the latest instalment in their Death Machines series of the 20th century's most successful assault weapons: the Oerlikon Anti-Aircraft Gun Paper Kit.

Created from flimsy card stock, this paper reproduction of a perennial Swiss bestseller – appropriated by all warring parties during WWI and WWII and still going strong to this day – incorporates 64 sheets of A0 paper. Infinitely more intricate and fragile than regular Airfix models, it transcends the mere nostalgia of boyhood fantasies to expose the irresistible pull and murky morality of wartime violence.

**POSTLERFERGUSON**
Ian Ferguson & Martin Postler
Oerlikon Anti Aircraft
*Part of PostlerFerguson's 'paper wars' series.*

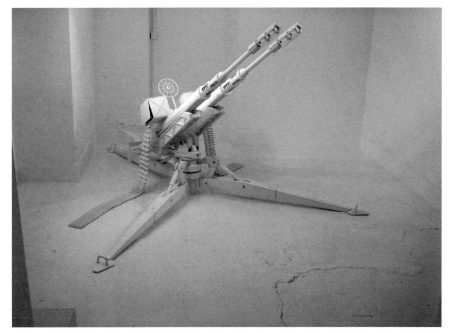

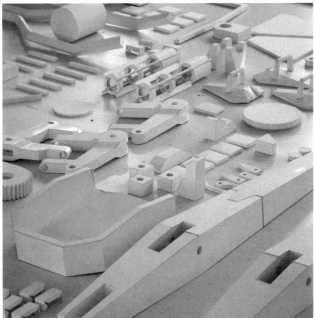

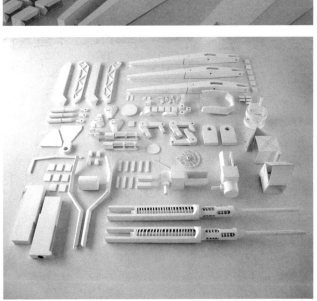

01

02

KENN MUNK

01 Antlor – The Deer Departed
DIY hunting trophies for the kind-
hearted (or vegetarian)! Spruce up
your den, cabin or glorious cubicle
with one of three limited edition
designs.

02 Yoyoyo Acapulco Antlor
Special Horsemoose version of
Ken Munk's paper Antlor for the
Norwegian band Yoyoyo Acapulco –
limited and numbered to 100.

## KENN MUNK

**03 Antlor – SecuriTV**

*A further social commentary by urban papercraft protagonist Ken Munk, SecuriTV takes his Antlor art to the next level. Here, the wall-mounted trophy comes back to haunt and surveil us – and the spectator becomes the hunted ...*

**04 Global Warning**

*With their future melting away almost as quickly as a mid-summer ice cream cone, Ken Munk's DIY polar bears serve to highlight the plight of endangered species around the globe. A limited edition of 100 paper kits, the unassembled sheets sport faux warning graphics to underline the urgency of global warming campaigns.*

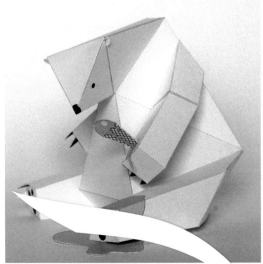

**SJORS TRIMBACH**
01 Speakerboss: CTR (Catch The Rainbow)
02 Speakerbooks

03 **ELOOLE**
Filomena

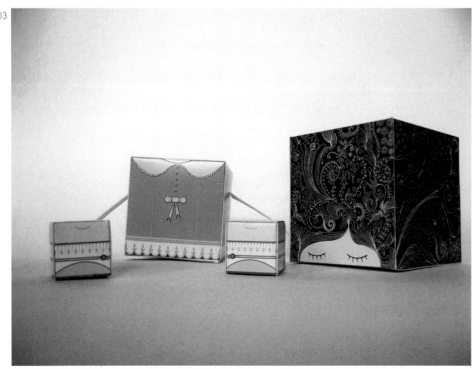

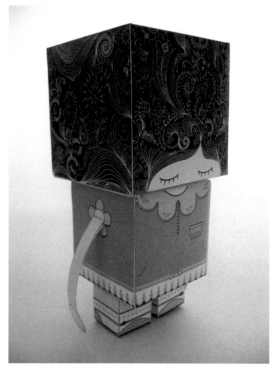

## MARSHALL ALEXANDER
04 <u>Bite Me</u>
05 <u>Marshall Alexander's papertoys</u>
06 <u>Foldskool Heroes series</u>

RICE FLAKES
Alimente seus monstros

02

Estão desaparecendo das prateleiras, e a gente garante que sem nenhuma ajuda dos mágicos.
havaianas kids

O trapezista só não pulou de alegria porque já tinha acabado o expediente.
havaianas kids

**CARLO GIOVANI**
01 Rice Flakes – feed your monsters
*Illustration for a promo poster.*

**CARLO GIOVANI ESTÚDIO**
**Agency: Almap BBDO**
02 Havaianas Kids
*Illustration for Havaianas Kids ads.*

**FWIS**
Corbis Readymech Cameras
03 Pablo
04 Dr. Livingstone
05 Photos of Your Mother
06 Peyote
07 Astrocam
*Readymech flatpack pinhole cameras – a promotional campaign for Corbis including flatpack paper pinhole cameras you can download, print, and build to make fully-functional cameras.*

03

04

05

06

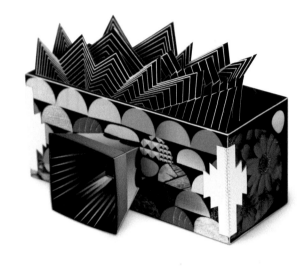

07

01

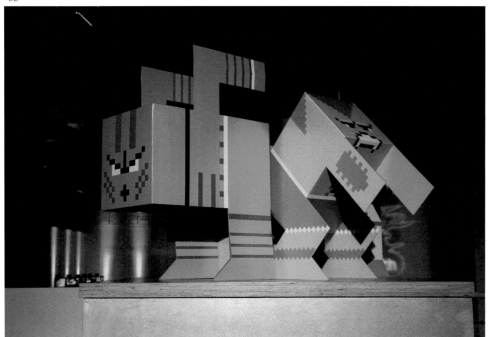

02

**FUPETE**
01 <u>iRobò @ Rialto 04</u>
*Installation & performance at
Rialtosantambrogio in Rome.*

**PAPER FOLDABLES**
**Bryan.**
02 <u>Giant Street Fighter Paper Foldables</u>
*Designed for CAPCOM's Street
Fighter brand.*
03 <u>My Michael Jackson Jacket</u>

03

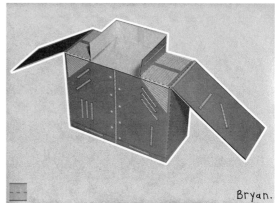

**PERRO LOCO**
04 Sleeper
05 Monster Munny
   *Munny (customised DIY toy) with*
   *cardboard head.*
06 Paper Spirits
07 Carlotta

**TUBBYPAWS**
08 Little Street With Vending Machines

**SJØRS TRIMBACH**
01 HF
02 boXer

**MARK JAMES**
03 CardBoy Cartridges
*Set of four: third series of
CardBoy figures.*

## MARK JAMES
### CardBoy Sneakers

*CardBoy, Mark James' "flat-packed freedom fighter", turns packaging inside out to reveal its true nature. "I wanted to go back to using cardboard as I was feeling a little guilty about the amount of plastic that was coming out of China."*

*Branded with their manufacturer's identity, these box-headed characters open up to reveal a body that flips around to form the final figure.*

*Joining a string of sneaker box playmates, James' four CardBoy Cartridges reference classic bubblejet ink cartridges to express his love of the Cyan (C), Magenta (M), Yellow (Y) and Black (K) printing process. Who needs 72dpi RGB when you can have the hard copy?*

## AKS/KWAN THUNG SENG
01 MR.SKULL
02 LOVE BIRD
03 Crossover Project for C2V
   *Prototype for comic book artist
   Michael Chuah aka C2V.*

01

02

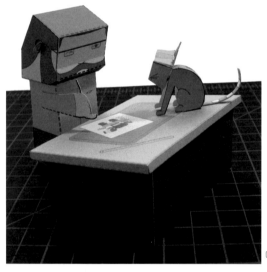

04

05

06

## BRIAN GUBICZA
**Template by Wilfried Villain**
04 E. A. Coobie (aka Paper Allan Poe)
   *Design by Brian Gubiza based on
   Wilfried Villain's Coobie Paper Toy
   template.*

## MATTHEW SHLIAN
05 Paper Matt

## MARK JAMES
06 Snyrd
   *Based on a sketch by Pete Fowler,
   Snyrd was created as a promotional
   item.*

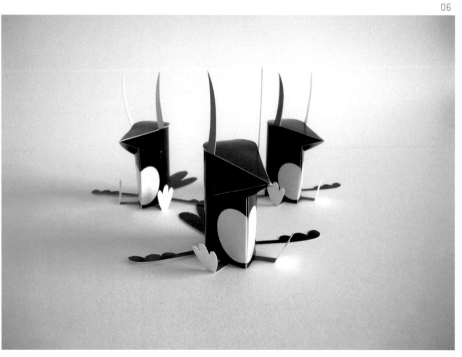

### NANIBIRD
**Josh McKible**

07 Anarchy Farmer
*Nanibird template and design by JoshMcKible.*

08 The Dears
*Done in collaboration with Ben the Illustrator. The Yes Dear model is based on Ben's Speakerdog template.*

09 **IVAN RICCI**
Chicchirichi
*Josh McKible's Nanibird customised by Ivan Ricci.*

10 **BRAINSTRIKERS ARTDENKA**
VooDooSKULL bird
*Customised by Artdenka.*

11 **AMY CARTWRIGHT**
Hoot Wink
*Customised by Amy Cartwright.*

### IVAN RICCI
**Template by Maarten Janssens**

12 Thai Ghost
*Thai Ghost from Phi Ta Khon, the Thai Ghost Festival. Design by Ivan Ricci based on Maarten Janssens BushDoctor template.*

13 Jagannatha
*In Hindu religion Jagannatha is the name of the Lord of the Universe. Design by Ivan Ricci based on Maarten Janssens 3EyedBear template.*

01

**BRIAN CASTLEFORTE**
01 NiceBunny Samurai HedKase
   *Part of HedKase series of paper toys.*
02 Riot Cop
   *Made for 'Sold Out' show hosted by Peel Magazine.*
03 NiceBunny paper toys

02

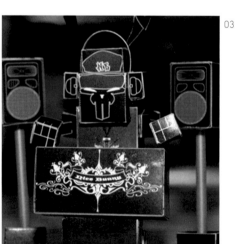

03

**MATT HAWKINS**
04 Snomoe
05 Comic Monkey
06 Wild Urp

**CHRISTOPHER BONNETTE**
07 La Catrina Chibi Paper Toy
   'Chibi Paper Toy' series.
   La Catrina is a representation of
   Death in Mexican folklore.
08 Squealers

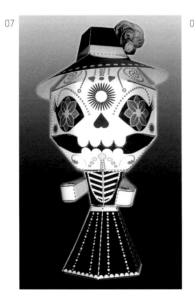

# ROCK AND ROLL CLOWN
unofficial fan-made free papertoy
boxpunx

boxpunx

series two
boxpunx
mods and tributes
2008jasonharlan
http://www.harlancore.com

**JASON HARLAN**
01 Rock n Roll Clown
*Based on a character from the
television show 'Metalocalypse'.*
02 Series Two – Mods & Tributes
03 Series Five – Punx in Space

JASON HARLAN
04 Series Four
05 Greyscale Terror
06 My Little Nny
   *Based on the character Johnny the Homicidal Maniac.*
07 The Strange One
   *Based on the character Emily.*

**BRIAN CASTLEFORTE**
01 Bruce Lee
   *Made for 'The Nature of Water –
   Bruce Lee' exhibition.*

**LOCOGRAFIX – PLAYROLL**
02 Fedde Le Grand – Output
   *Papertoy made for DJ & producer
   Fedde Le Grand's album Output.*

**DIRK BEHLAU**
03 The Pixeleye Papertoy
   *In collaboration with Illunatic.*

03

ANGELLO GARCÍA BASSI / CUBOTOY

04 Sandy Jr.
05 Sleepy Sandy
   *Using clothing designs by*
   *Sandy Clothing.*
06 Javiera Mena
   *Javiera Mena is a Chilean singer.*
07 Darth Paper
   Joe
08 The God Eye
09 Cuboboy / Selfportrait

SHIN TANAKA
Three

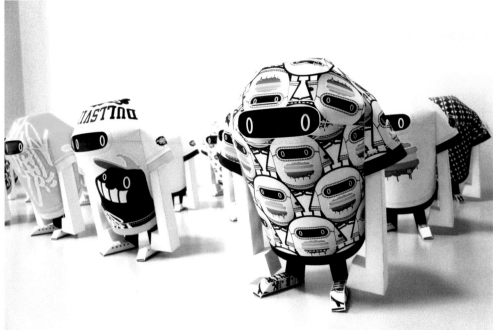

02

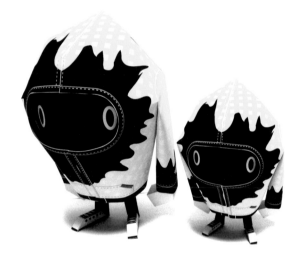

03

SHIN TANAKA
01 T-BOY
02 Hoophy

SHIN TANAKA X GIANT ROBOT X SCION
03 4-in-1 robot

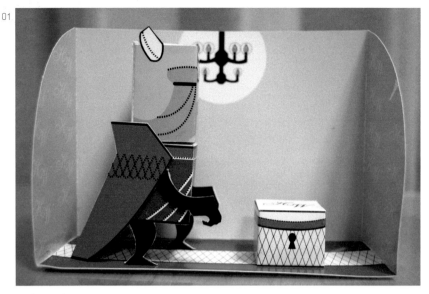

**HORRORWOOD**
01 Retro Demon
02 Toro Oscuro
03 A Bad Dream on Birch Street
   Dark Lord & Steed
04 Ghosts in the Machine

**MARKO ZUBAK**
05 Samurai
06 Rebelde

*right page:*
**SJORS TRIMBACH & SERGEY SAFONOV**
Nosferatula
*Custom made for the Stikova project in Moscow. Figure by Sergey Safonov, customised by Sjors Trimbach.*

**CARLO GIOVANI ESTÚDIO**
Carlo Giovani, Heitor Yida,
Ligia Jeon, Fabiano Silva,
Rodrigo Silveira, Adriana Komura
Mundos Invisíveis
*Stop motion animation.*

*While his "Rice Flakes – feed your monsters" animation finds a city waking up as the objects of their own nightmares, Giovani's contribution to TV documentary 'Mundos Invisíveis' follows a more enlightened path.*

*A 20-minute rollercoaster ride through time and human ingenuity, Giovani's articulated paper protagonists retrace the steps of those who researched what really matters: matter itself.*

*From Aristotle to Heraclitus, from Paracelsus to Einstein, the lively stop-motion adventure takes us into the makeshift labs of physicists, alchemists, chemists and mathematicians from ancient Greece to the present day.*

*Painstakingly photographed, frame by frame, with a pinch of nostalgia and Tim Burton-esque aesthetics, Giovani's stop-motion masterpiece conveys the undiluted delight of discovery and illumination.*

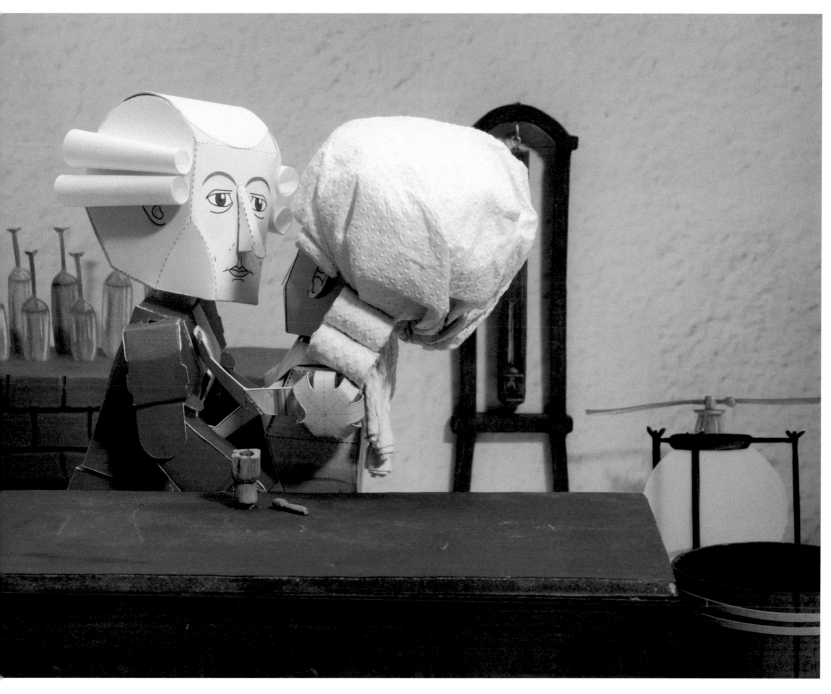

CARLO GIOVANI ESTÚDIO
01 Paper Nature
Illustration created for the Souza
Cruz Institute.

CARLO GIOVANI ESTÚDIO
Carlo Giovani & Bruno Algarve
02 Elma Chips Kids
Stop motion animation for Elma
Chips Kids.

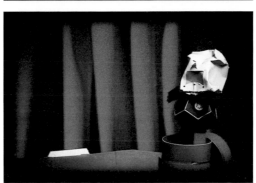

**CARLO GIOVANI ESTÚDIO**
Carlo Giovani & Bruno Algarve
03 Gordo Freak Show
*Stop motion animation for the opening of the Brazilian MTV talk show 'Gordo Freak Show'.*

**BENT IMAGE LAB**
Rob Shaw
04 They Might Be Giants 'I'm Impressed'
*Music video for They Might be Giants song I'm Impressed.*

04

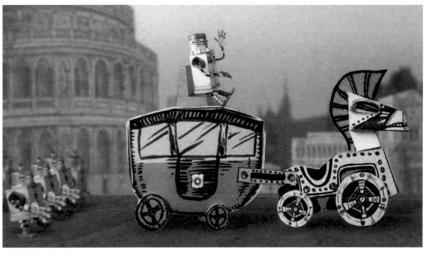

01

02

03

CARLO GIOVANI ESTÚDIO
Carlo Giovani, Ligia Jeon, Heitor Yida,
Adriana Komura, Fabiano Silva
01 São Jorge and the Dragon

CARLO GIOVANI
02 Night shot
03 Winter
04 Samurai
*Originally created as an illustration
for Supereinteressante magazine.*

# Bespoke reinvention

FASHION / COSTUME

Originally a shameful substitute for more lasting materials in periods of war and crisis, from flimsy cardboard shoes to cheap paper collars, in the 1960s, paper enjoyed a more fashionable revival.

Kick-started by the surprise success of a Scott Paper company giveaway, simple paper dresses soon achieved true cult status – and equally proud price tags. In the spirit of anything goes and economic exuberance, the crisp, clean lines of paper garments captured the public's imagination with their futuristic, space age appeal and inspired artists and designers from Andy Warhol to Paco Rabanne.

Bridging the gap between avant-garde decadence and pragmatic necessity, the colourful, pop-art inspired trend soon crossed the Atlantic - and Iron Curtain – as a cheap and cheerful East German summer substitute. Surviving up to five bouts in the washing machine, the gorgeously flimsy affairs invited wear, tear and unceremonious alteration. Just snip to fit – and throw away.

Although their papery weakness emphasised the previously disdained notion of ephemeral fashion, of disposable designs for a season or two, their affordable availability in times of shortage appeased the ideological powers in charge.

A perennial favourite with designers from John Galliano to Ann Demeulemeester – especially those with a penchant for more abstract, geometric exercises, like Issey Miyake or Hussein Chalayan as well as more rebellious souls like Jum Nakao, whose collection was torn apart during the show – paper fashion has come a long way since its functional outings as tie and dress.

Now valued for its frailty and decay, its potential for fragile fragmentation, paper likes to advertise and emphasise its own unsuitability for everyday attire. Like a vinyl recording that degrades a little with every play, today's paper clothing (or its longer-lasting synthetic cousin, Tyvek) embraces its own perishability – every wear, every wash adds to its disintegration, makes it softer and more delicate, until it begins to fray at the edges.

Flitting between illustration and masquerade, the works assembled in this chapter appropriate this take on brittle fragility, of paper's intrinsic unwearability, to explore the idea of fashion itself – how the clothes that we choose can adorn, hide, expose or change us.

Mapping the future of fashion itself, Elisabeth Lecourt's geographic dresses retrace their wearer's life in the city, while others prefer to play hide and seek with the notion of our identity: From doily-laced paper illustrations and chic cutouts that juxtapose striking styles with stylised backdrops to deliberately enigmatic, encompassing narratives, every slice and stitch tells a story.

Here, well-crafted stages and 2D/3D illusions blur the boundaries between life and set, between real and surreal to let the paper take centre stage, with humans relegated to mere decoration. In a formal variant of a perennial seaside favourite, we push heads and arms through well-hidden holes to try on a new body and self, from stiff-collared 17th century Madame to sassy yet subdued 1950s maiden. By prescribing the range of movements and poses, it is the clothes that carry and "wear" the person, dictating their posture and physical expression.

Those with a more sinister streak revisit the theme of court jester and fool – and the dubious honour of being king for a day – with carnivalesque, sculpted paper masks and attire. Taken to the extreme of geometric abstraction, these modifications can lead to the obliteration of the visible self – and thus a new bout of personal reinvention.

BELA BORSODI
Alto Profilo
*Editorial for Elle Magazine, Italy.*

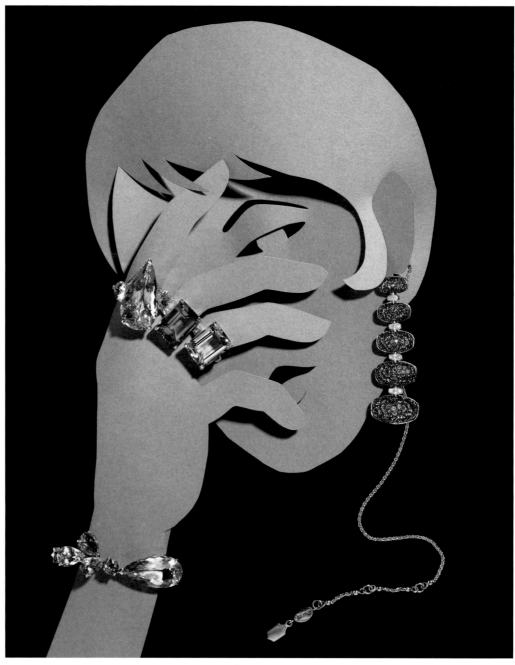

### BELA BORSODI

01 <u>Alto Profilo</u>
*Editorial for Elle Magazine, Italy.*
02 <u>Girl</u>
*Editorial for Tatler, Russia.*
03 <u>Shoezoo</u>
*Editorial for Kid's Wear, Germany.*

*Austrian fashion still-life photographer Bela Borsodi excels at the art of contradicting himself.*

*Ripping objects and models from their familiar surroundings, he restages fashion and accessories in his own controlled context. Akin to miniature sets, his crafted backdrops breathe life into static items, emphasise his "stars'" sculptural qualities – and add a generous dash of saucy humour to the mix.*

*Here, Borsodi's distinct, yet neutral backdrops for baubles and accessories offset the items' striking styles against the stylised chic of monochrome cutouts and silhouettes.*

*Emerging from straightforward construction card, these basic props are then cut and shifted – against their own tresses, folds and features – to inject some life, movement and depth into the otherwise level playing field. For a taste of Borsodi's more outlandish scenes, check out his sets made from wire, balloons, raw meat or suntan lotion.*

01

02

03

04

05

06

## ELISABETH LECOURT

<u>Les Robes Géographiques</u>

*As a cartographer uses maps to describe the world we live in, Lecourt turns them into personal items of clothing that represent the wearer's habitat and identity.*

01 <u>Bâteaux sur l'Eau</u>
*Map of the United Kingdom.*
02 <u>Rouge Gorge</u>
*Map of the London underground.*
03 <u>Ainsi Fanf Font Font</u>
*Map of Paris.*
04 <u>Un Petit Tour</u>
*Map of Paris.*
05 <u>Sat On The Wall</u>
*Map of Tibet.*
06 <u>Les Petits poissons</u>
*Map of San Francisco.*
07 <u>Fanfan la Tulipe</u>
*Map of New York.*
08 <u>A La Queue Leuleu</u>
*Map of New York.*
09 <u>Bumblebee</u>
*Map of the Mount Blanc.*

07

08

09

SILJA GOETZ
Goddess

01

02

03

**EVELINA BRATELL**
01 Jane Doe
02 Ms Sour
03 With title
04 Ms Sweet

**CHRISTIAN TAGLIAVINI**
Dame di Cartone
01 Cubism II
02 17th Century II
03 Cubism III
04 Dame di Cartone / 17th Century I

*right page:*

**CHRIS HEADS**
–

01

02

03

**MACOTO SAITO**
01 Eriko
02 Wind Venus

**RICHARD SWEENEY**
03 Figure
*Using cardboard salvaged from bins, a figure was produced at full human scale with flexible joints for posing.*

## POLLY VERITY

04 Paper Dress
05 Paper Helmet and Jerkin

*Curved folds in the paper cause the developable surface to curl up in an intriguing way. This effect is used to make paper garments and dresses.*

## POLLY VERITY & TOM VERITY

06 Masque

04

*In their formal abstraction between mask and myth, fashion and sculpture, Polly Verity's paper dresses, helmets, jerkins and skirts exaggerate the carnivalesque, masquerading qualities of human attire.*

*Blurring the boundaries between wearable and unwearable, between pleated garment and mathematical thought experiment, the enforced stiff posturing underlines the performative aspect of Verity's creations.*

*One step further into the realm of fashion and fantasy – at the Comme des Garçons flagship store on London's Dover Street – her intricate geometric folds and pleats manifest as miniature mythological creatures, itching to escape the confines of their papery skins.*

05

06

01

02

04

I am
bursting
with joy.

03

POLLY VERITY
01 Snarling mask

PIXELGARTEN
02 Um was es nicht geht

KEETRA DEAN DIXON
03 Overjoyed
   Postcard

CARL KLEINER
04 Ceremony

DONNIE LUU
Black Helmets
*Collection of five helmets made with the technique of modular origami. The helmets are each made of 30–40 square sheets of paper, folded into units that connect together to create an abstracted geometric form. The helmets were used in 2008 for a live performance by Collabo, a Los Angeles based visual performance group.*

01

**AKATRE**

01 Friendly Fires
   *Picture of the rock band Friendly
   Fires for French magazine Tsugi.*

**JEREMIAS BÖTTCHER**

02 Papstars
   *Music video for Jazalou and
   Lockefella.*

02

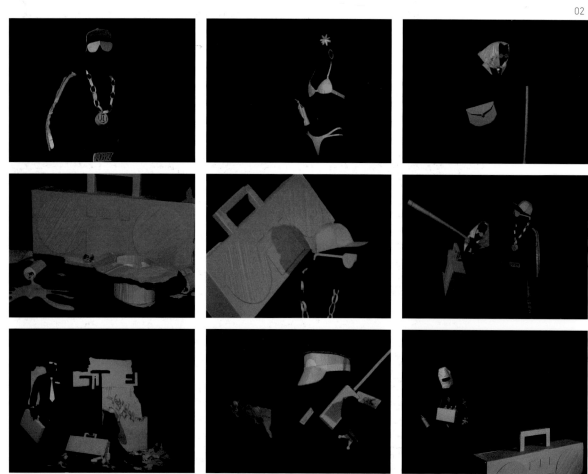

03

04

**AKATRE**
03 <u>Kreyol Factory, La Villette</u>
04 <u>'Je pense comme une fille enlève</u>
   <u>sa robe'</u>
   *Visual for a choregraphic show*
   *shown during the dance festival*
   *'Faits d'hiver'.*

**TOYKYO**
05 Benjamin Van Oost
   <u>Ride a horse</u>
   *Costume for Edelweiss studio.*

05

**LUCYANDBART**
01 Exploded View
02 Spring

01

02

*right page:*
**AKATRE**
Mains d'Œuvres
*Visual for a theatre show.*

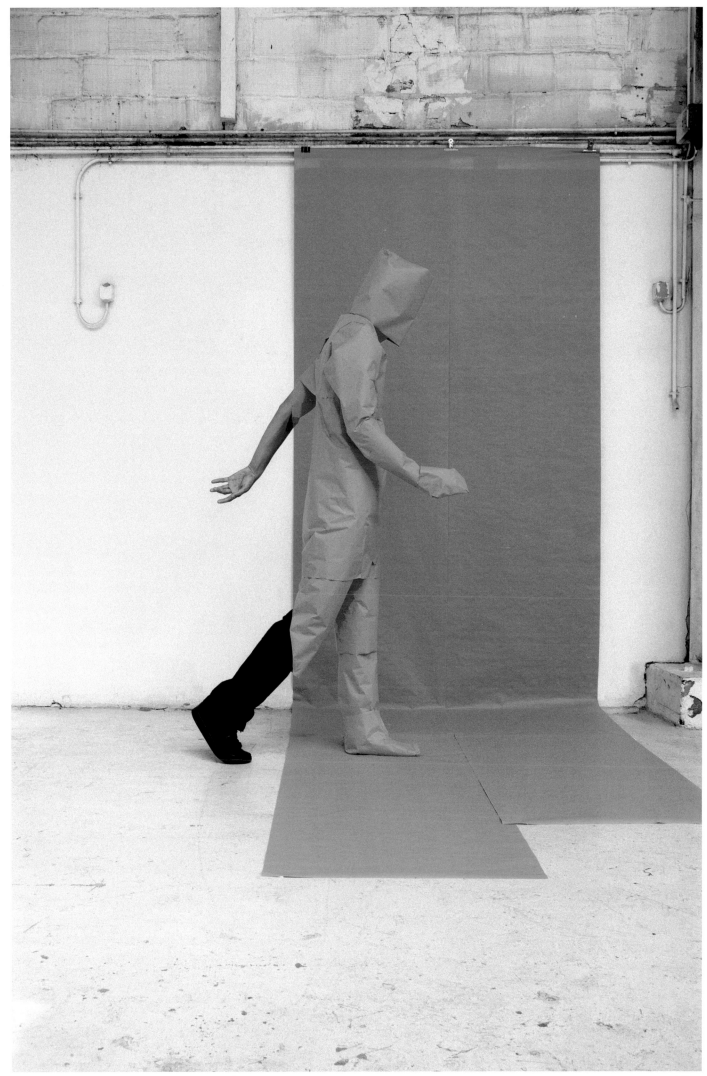

### AKATRE
Mains d'Œuvres
Visuals for music concerts and
bi-monthly programme posters.

Simple, stark and effective, Paris-
based graphic design trio Akatre love
a bit of drama – and the world of
performance arts. From high art to
lowbrow rock, their designs for art,
music and theatre events replace our
everyday routines with a healthy dose
of perspective-altering visual escapism.

Trailing their protagonists, we follow
Akatre from plain white into pink – or
straight into the striking alienation of
their Mains d'Oeuvres series of poster
installations. Here, scale ceases to matter: Akatre's (un)willing participants
find themselves entangled in paper,
caught up in giant sheets, cuts and folds,
to be devoured by their surroundings.

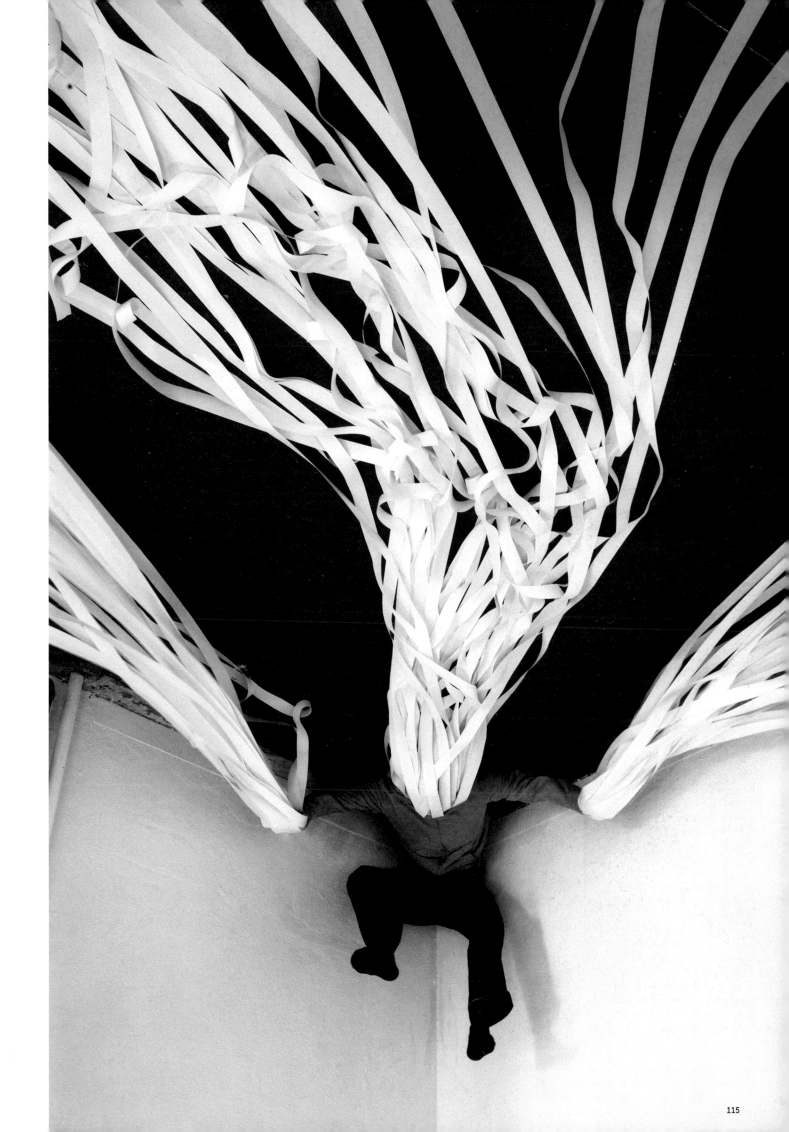

*left page:*
**KIYOSHI KURODA**
Black Butterfly

**CONTAINERPLUS**
The Evil Twins - The Writer's Story
*Self initiated project.*

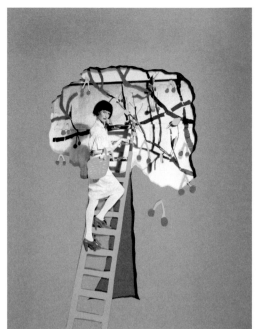

IJM
Karin Nussbaumer, Frank Visser
Paper Garden

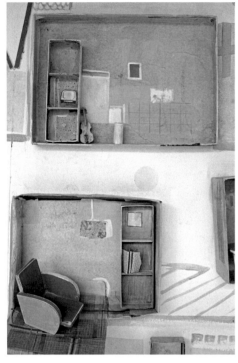

**KERSTIN ZU PAN**
01 Paper Doll
02 Paper

Kerstin zu Pan's deliberately enigmatic, dreamlike creations explore "beauty in unusual circumstances". Like stills from stories never told, the resulting images are expressive, ambitious, over-the-top – and always out of this world.

Infused with a touch of 1980s camp, the depicted work stages explosions of paper, people and paint in a series of expressionist collages for a strangely pristine play on the themes of indulgence and gluttony.

Aiding and abetting zu Pan, artist Yuka Oyama and wig creator Acacio da Silva help set the scene for this innocently sinful staged adventure.

# 02

# _Shapes and Guises_

_POP-UP / BOOK / LAYERS / OBJECTS_

Where is up and where is down? And does it even matter? Emerging from the flatness of a simple A4 sheet, from lightweight stock or heavy card, fragile thought experiments escape their humble origins to take charge of the space around them, to give us a glimpse of the secret machinations and intricate folds that lie within.

Over the course of the following chapter, from lacy silhouettes to towering castles and literary constructs, paper goes from strength to strength as a versatile material for artwork and sculptures.

Many of the objects and three-dimensional tableaux in question toy with the markers of heritage and culture, of shadow and light, of shifting views and teetering perspectives to reveal new angles and insights depending on the spectator's position. A prime example of this approach, Olof Bruce's interpretation of Italo Calvino's 'Invisible Cities', toggles surface and underground, order and chaos, the rough and the smooth, according to our subjective reference point.

In a different take on light, space and magic, Ju Jordy Fu's chandelier mobiles illuminate the darker sides of human life. Pulled down – and into existence – by their own weight, they betray their man-made origin, albeit with a skewed, dreamlike quality that suggests a constant rearrangement of facts and factors.

Similar to these unfolding objects, the chapter itself opens up to encompass ever more interactive concoctions. While Ingrid Siliakus takes pop-ups to new and architectural heights, others add a generous pinch of POP to the technique's underlying principle.

In their reappropriation of printed matter, contributors from Robert The to Brian Dettmer prove that books are not untouchable relics, but eminently suitable for artistic recycling. Often mere symbols of the ideas they represent rather than true conveyors of content, outdated tomes receive new relevance in a range of destructive/constructive reinterpretations. From The's "sweeping statement", to Jacqueline Rush Lee's "Phoenix-from-the-Ashes"-like blossoming blooms, these book lovers cut, crumple, burn or dye away all nonessential information to lay bare the guts of their source medium in a range of complex, three-dimensional sculptures.

What is left after this aesthetic anatomy session amounts to a truly visceral experience, delving deep into seamed stratifications to unearth the visual gems and encrustations left behind on the book's inside walls. Similar, albeit more colourful and stringent striations reappear in the works of Jen Stark who stacks her mesmerising petals and vortices into 3D sculptures of paper perfection.

From slashed layers to manifestations of higher geometry, a number of mathematical explorers try their hand at spiky polyhedrons, at undiscovered viruses and complex protein structures, in a string of multidimensional thought experiments. Finally, where math meets magic, we encounter the mythical creatures and wireframe teddies of Polly Verity and Ryuji Nakamura: abstract vessels, yet to be filled with a toddler's – or adult's – sense of wonder.

_right page:_
PETER CALLESEN
Cowboy (detail)

**HINA AOYAMA**
Forest of heart
*Scissor-cut paper.*

*Paper and patience is all she needs – with the steady hand of a practised surgeon, Hina Aoyama snips away at her intricate art to reveal the gossamer threads of poetry in motion.*

*In their subdued subtlety, Aoyama's super-fine lacy cuttings emphasise the beauty of restraint and submission, brought to a head in her painstaking typographical homage to Baudelaire's Les Fleurs du Mal.*

*By submitting to this lengthy labour of love, Aoyama embodies and visualises the spirit of her subject matter.*

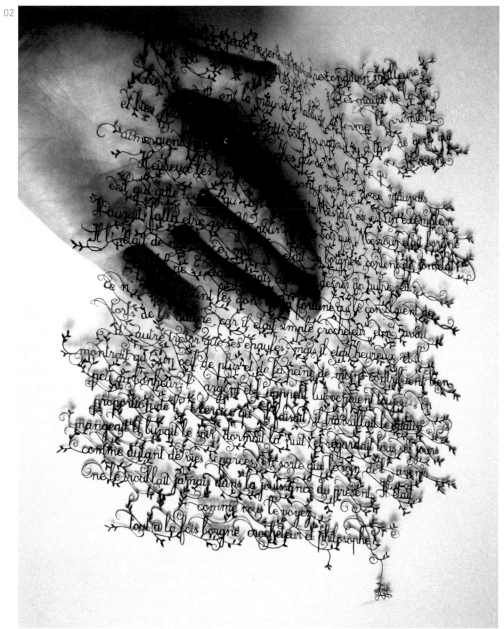

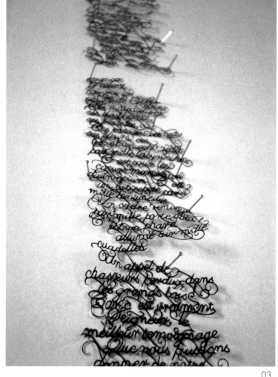

**HINA AOYAMA**
01 Héron and Camellia
02 Lettre de Voltaire
03 'Les Phares' in Baudelaire's
'Fleurs du mal'
*Scissor-cut paper.*

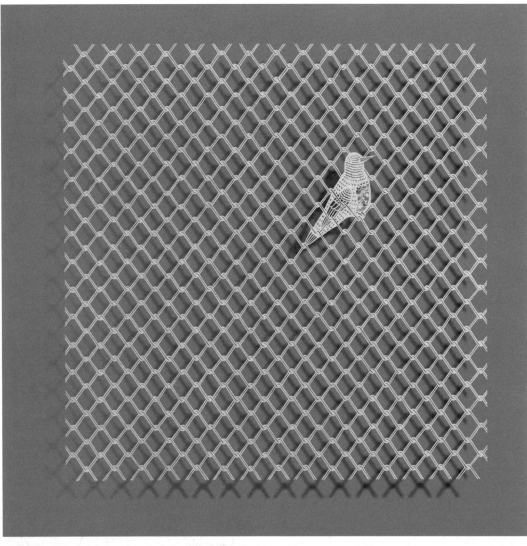

**BOVEY LEE**
01 Little Crimes
02 Office Tornado
03 Tsunami

A native of Hong Kong, Bovey Lee combines East and West in her blade-cut illustrations. Reviving the ancient Chinese folk art of rice paper cut-outs, now threatened by rapid modernisation, she replaces folklore and mystical creatures with personal narratives, current affairs, politics and gender issues.

Often hanging by the finest sliver, these fragile filigrees emphasise the material's delicate translucency, offset against her subjects' upside-down worlds. "I glide the tip of the blade over the rice paper like a brush, a method from my calligraphy and painting background. Although the hand-cutting demands extreme concentration and fastidiousness, it is also an immensely gratifying and spiritual experience."

Transcending geographies, cultures and time, the webbed interconnectedness of her tableaux reflects the juxtaposition and embrace of both Eastern and Western compositional approaches, including bilateral symmetry, modular patterns and symbolic figuration.

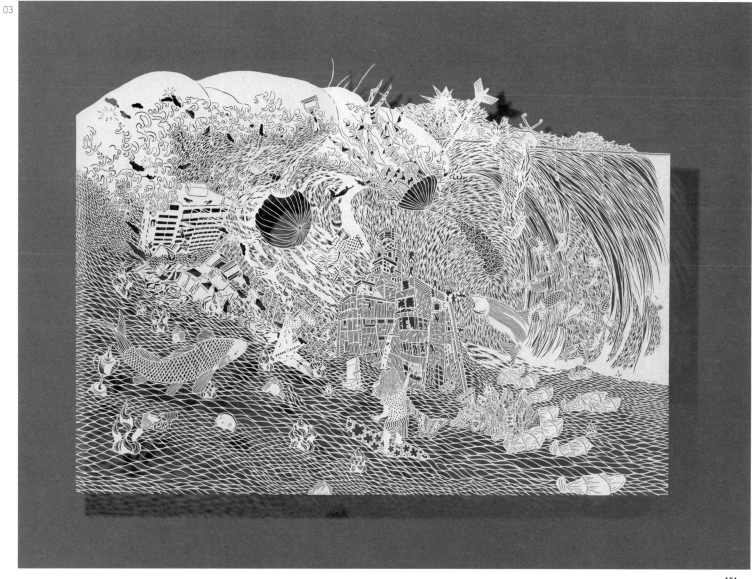

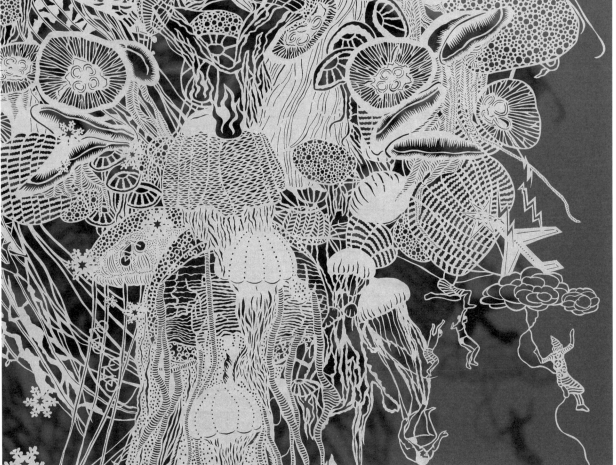

BOVEY LEE
01 Tsunami (details)
02 Atomic Jellyfish (details)

*right page:*
BOVEY LEE
Atomic Jellyfish

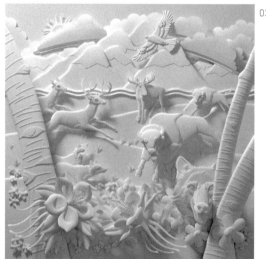

**JEFF NISHINAKA**

01 <u>Jackie Chan Drunken Master</u>
Sculpture commissioned by Jackie
Chan for personal collection.

02 <u>El Sereno Phœnix</u>
Sculpture for the main lobby of the
Barrio Action Youth & Family Center
in El Sereno, California.

03 <u>Preserve</u>
Sculpture for Sprint Press,
Denver CO.

Two decades ago, Jeff Nishinaka
discovered a then unconventional
sculpting material – paper. "I was look-
ing for something that would set me
apart from the rest of the crowd. So,
I grabbed an X-Acto blade and started
slicing. From the first cut, it felt good!"

Carefully chopped, layered and
glued, the material comes to life under
Nishinaka's skilled fingers. At first
glance, the resulting reliefs might
pass for neoclassical plaster of Paris
murals, for standout examples of
European flair of post-Soviet grandeur.

Take a closer look, and the subject matter reveals its topical and
transnational nature: from expansive
American sports hall to Jackie Chan's
iconic Drunken Master, in a sozzled
Monkey pose (a commission by the
Drunken Master himself), Nishinaka
depicts the world around him – in all
its flawed glory.

**JEFF NISHINAKA**

04 <u>Sports Hall</u>
05 <u>Beaver Stadium</u>

*The Sports Hall and the Beaver Stadium sculpture were photographed and printed onto wall paper and then applied to the interior wall of the PSU All-Sports Museum located in the southwest corner of Beaver Stadium at Penn State University.*

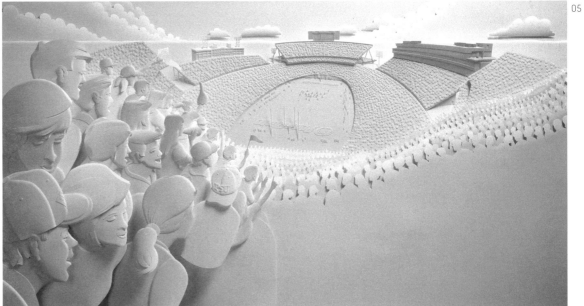

# 05

PETER CALLESEN
01 <u>Birds trying to escape their drawings
(detail)</u>
02 <u>Distant Wish</u>

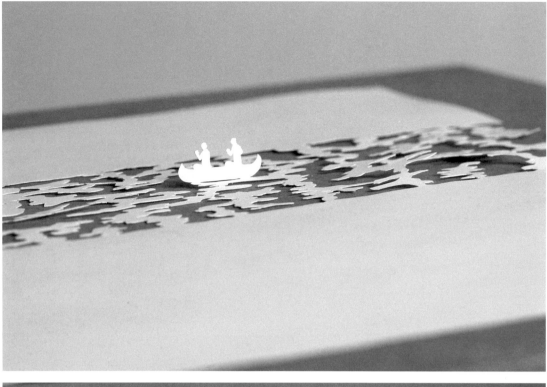

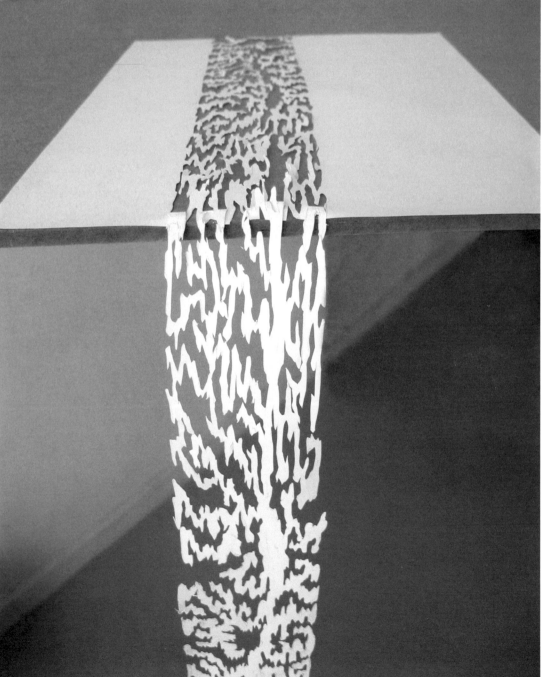

## PETER CALLESEN

01 Eismeer
02 Down the River

A perennial paper art favourite and masterful narrator, Peter Callesen requires just a few snips to change his story, to tweak our perceptions of tragedy and redemption.

Stark, but never simplistic, he delights in adding by taking away; in exploring the binaries of black and white, front and back, up and down, death and rebirth, positive and negative space.

From the untouched surface of ordinary A4 paper, a narrative arises. Or rather, lots of them.

What emerges from this pristine substrate enters a new, interdependent unit with the remaining sheet, eternally tied to its paper origins. This story of fetters, of being tied to our roots, remains a recurring theme in Callesen's work.

Taken to the extreme with his precarious castles and cityscapes, Callesen delights in the "aesthetic of possible failure – always on the verge of collapsing, of falling apart or being flattened by an awkward hand."

## PETER CALLESEN

01 <u>Human Ruin</u>
02 <u>Tall Tower of Babel</u>
03 <u>Big Paper Castle</u>
   *Cut and folded from one piece
   of paper.*

**YU JORDY FU**
01 Cloud Chandelier – Family
*The Cloud Chandelier – Family was exhibited at the 'Don't Panic' exhibition at the Yard Gallery, London, UK*
02 Family®
*Masterplan and architectural design for Eastern Quarry in Dartford, UK*
03 Cloud Lamp Collection 2009
04 Cloud Lamp Milan

02

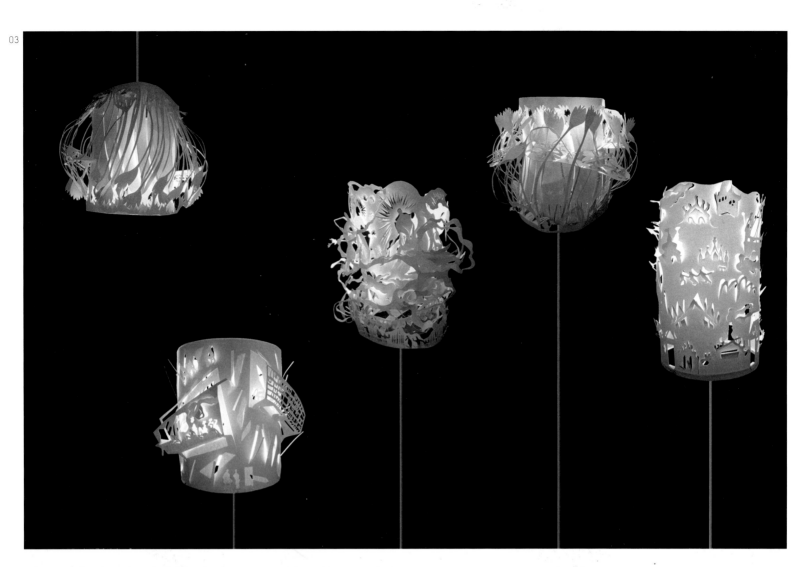

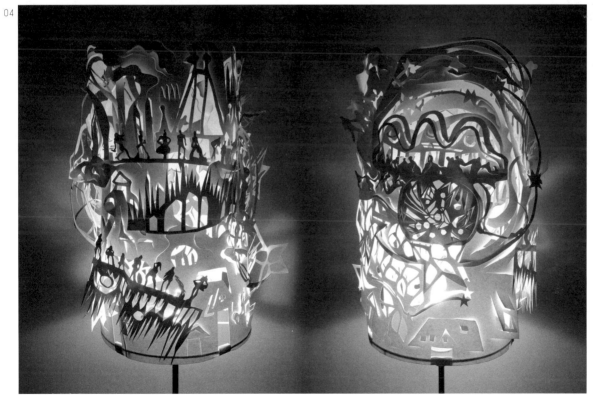

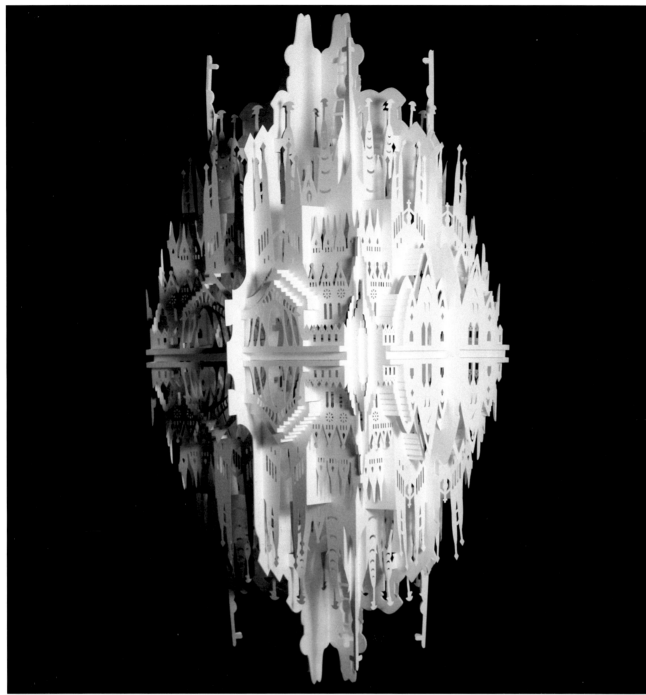

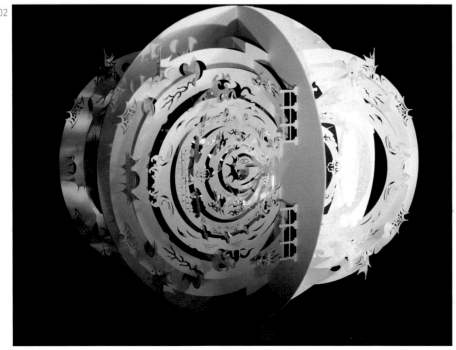

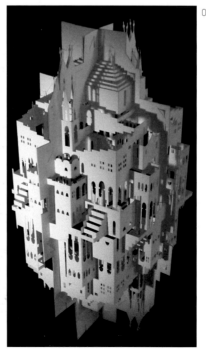

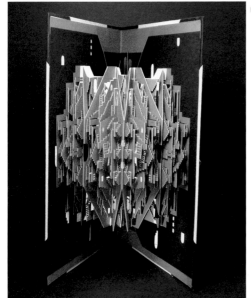

04

**INGRID SILIAKUS**

01 Reflection on Sagrada Familia
*Inspired by Antoni Gaudi's work 'Sagrada Familia', the artwork consists of eight individual sides: four outer and four interior elements. All of these segments are cut and folded out of a single piece of paper. Opened up, these sides provide a glimpse on the inside artwork. The entire object may be folded down into a two-dimensional flat pack.*

02 Innerrings

03 Reflection

**INGRID SILIAKUS**

04 Stairsmapping
*Abstract with architectonic characteristics. The artwork consists of three differently coloured layers. Each layer is cut and folded from a single piece of paper. Each opening displays a different interaction between the layers.*

05 Reflejar

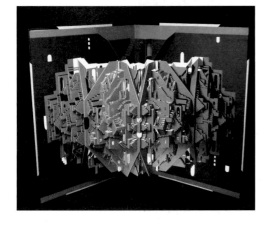

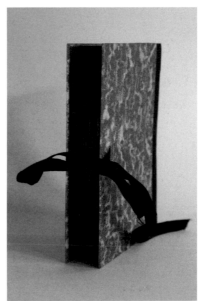

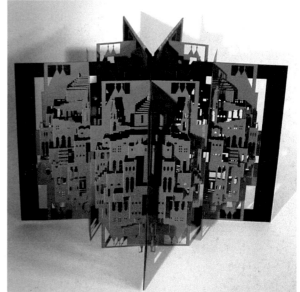

05

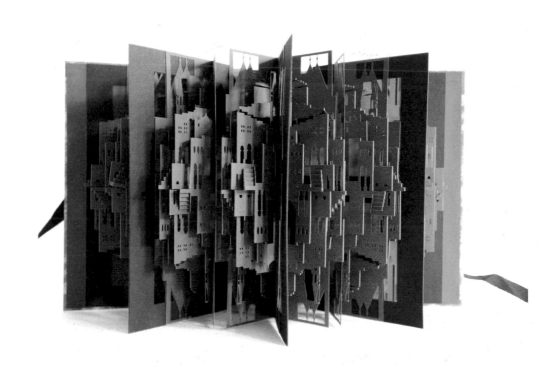

**OLOF BRUCE, TOM ERIKSSON &
LIV WADSTRÖM**
Invisible Cities

*This book is an artistic interpretation of Italo Calvino's 'Invisible Cities'. A pop-up book illustrating surface and underground, order and chaos, glossy and rough.*

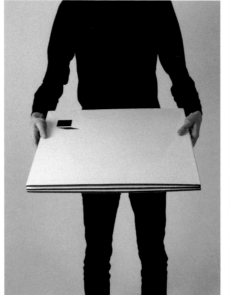

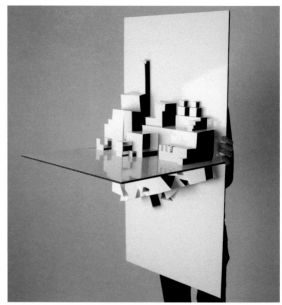

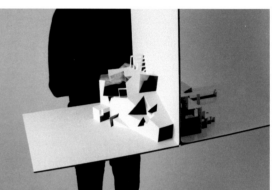

**OLOF BRUCE, TOM ERIKSSON &
LIV WADSTRÖM**
Invisible Cities

*This book is an artistic interpretation of 'Invisible Cities'. A pop-up book illustrating surface and underground, order and chaos, glossy and rough.*

# 01

# COLETTE FU

<u>Haunted Philadelphia Series</u>

*Series of 10 photographic pop-up books created while in residence at the Provincetown Fine Arts Work Center, Massachusetts.*

*As Philadelphia is a 'City of Firsts' for its historic sites and centuries-old buildings, it has become known as one of America's most haunted cities. The pop-up books highlight selected predicaments of this East Coast metropolis.*

01 <u>Boathouse Row</u>
02 <u>Byberry Mental Hospital</u>
03 <u>Eastern State Penetentiary, Cellblock 12</u>
04 <u>Rodin Museum</u>

**JULIEN VALLÉE & BLEUBLANCROUGE**
01 Black & White teaser
*Stop motion video created for a division of Bleublancrouge Montreal's agency Black & White.*

**ASIF MIAN / EVAQ**
02 Aesop Rock 'Fast Cars'
*Stop motion music video for 'Fast Cars' by Aesop Rock.*

02

03

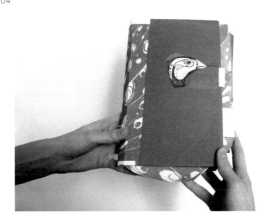

04

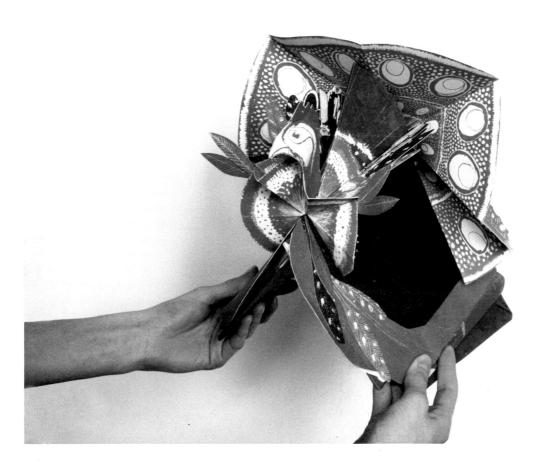

01

02

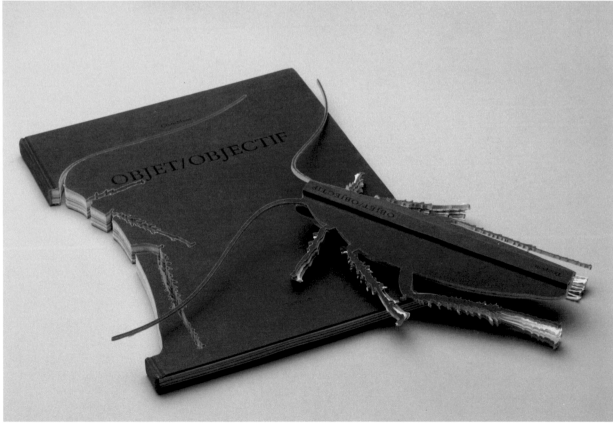

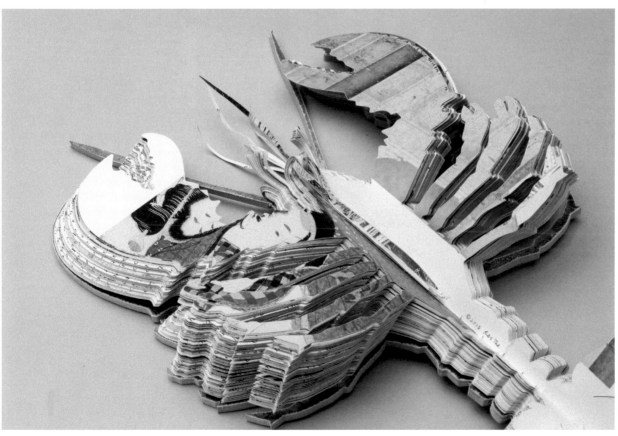

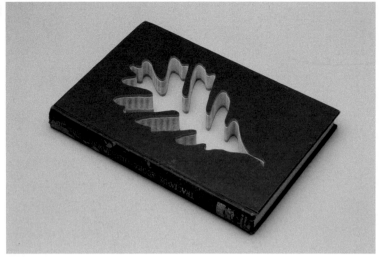

**ROBERT THE**

01 Tractatus
02 Encyclopaedia Britannica Volume 14
03 Glasses

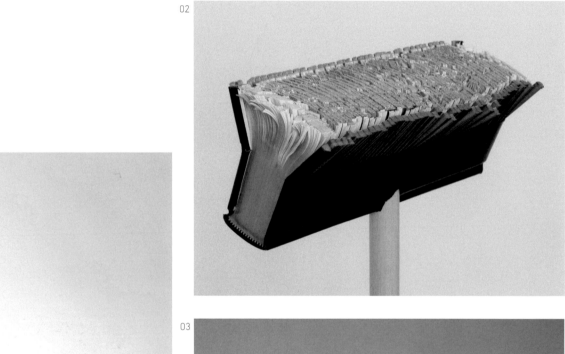

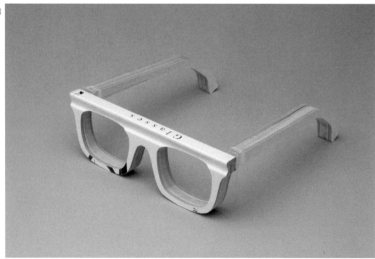

**LISA OCCHIPINTI**
Book Mobile
04 Exiles
05 Chocolate Days
06 The Silent World

04

**JACQUELINE RUSH LEE**
Volumes Series
*For this series, water was used to
transform the books further.*
07 Stack
08 Book of R's
09 Cube

07

**JACQUELINE RUSH LEE**

Devotion Series
01 Anthologia
02 Flutter
03 Unfurled
04 Unfurled II
*In this series, the covers are layered with inks, sanded to reveal inner layers and then burnished.*

Ex Libris Series
05 Unfurled
06 Shrunken Encyclopedia
*Books high fired in kiln through experimental firing process.*

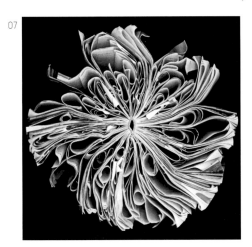

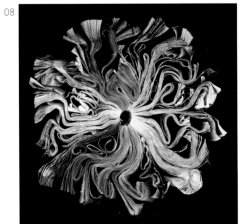

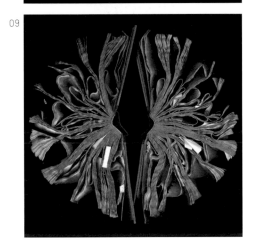

CARA BARER

07 Ms.
08 Carmen
   *Houston Yellow Pages Phone Book.*
09 Roget's
   *Roget's Thesarus, molded with water.*
10 Homage to Chamberlin
   *Phone Book molded with water.*

01

 04

 05

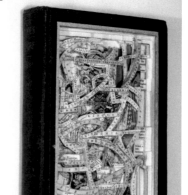 02

 03

**BRIAN DETTMER**
01 World Science
02 Modern Progress
03 Pattern Layouts
04 The Connoisseur's Complete Guide
05 Complete Book of Ballets

*Dust off those old tomes!*

*In his alteration of existing media, Brian Dettmer uncovers new relevance in the irrelevant. His capable hands carve new meaning and aesthetics out of outdated books, maps and periodicals to reveal an alternative view or interpretation.*

*Akin to a sculptor, who "sees" the exact lines and curves in a block of marble, there is no going back after the first cut – yet by slicing away all non-essentials, Dettmer creates a skeletal, yet infinitely deeper version of the pragmatic original, a Vernean "journey to the centre of the earth" filled with curious wonders.*

*These rich and rewarding "book autopsies" – some of them folded, stacked or sanded to resemble geological formations or blocks of wood – offer the best possible proof that books are not untouchable relics, but eminently suitable raw materials for recycling and reappropriation.*

07

06

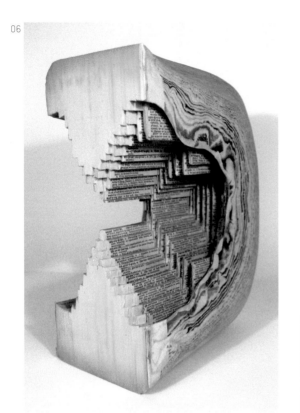

08

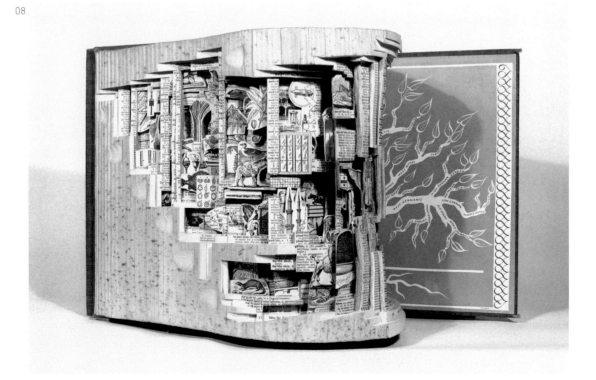

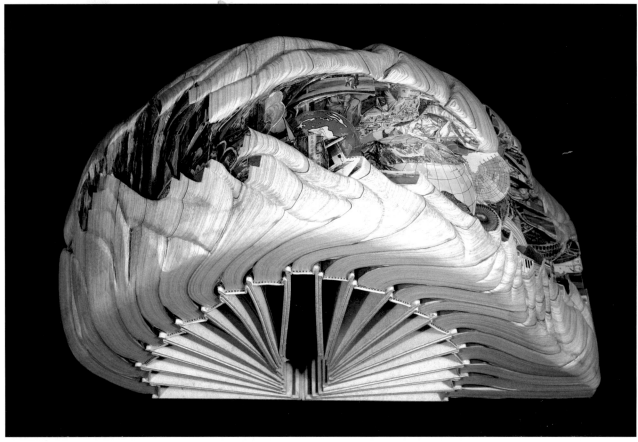

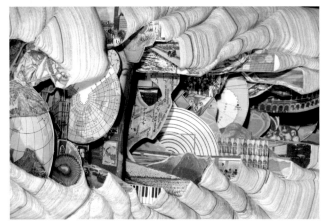

**BRIAN DETTMER**

01 <u>New Books of Knowledge</u>
02 <u>Full Set of Funk</u>
   *Altered set of encyclopedias con-
   nected, formed, sanded, sealed and
   carved.* ‒

2

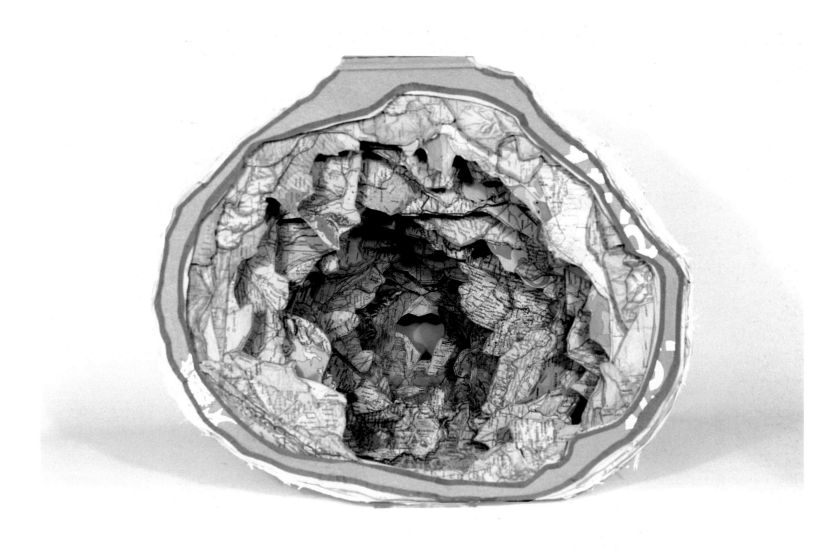

**BRIAN DETTMER**
Prevent Horizon
*Altered atlases, carved and connected.*

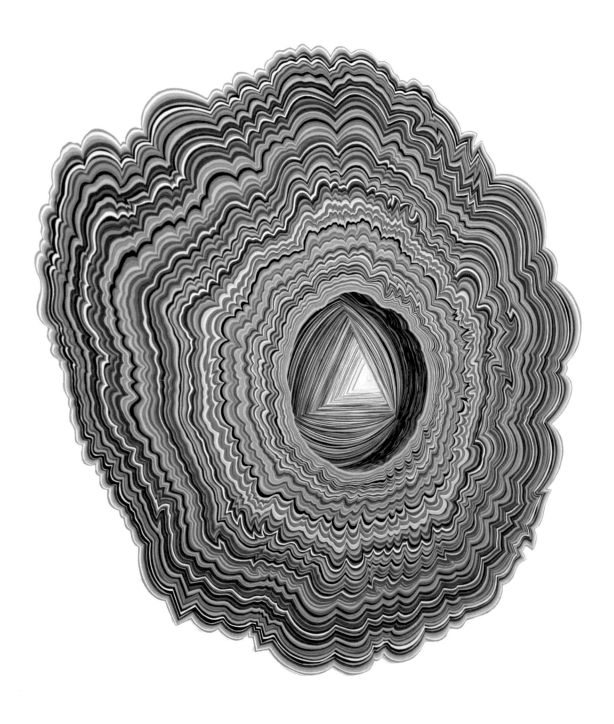

**JEN STARK**
Microscopic Entry

A proponent of the 'virtue out of necessity' school, Jen Stark's mesmerisingly complex works might never have come into being – if not for a study trip to France. "I only took two suitcases with me, so there was no room for art supplies. On arrival, I made my way to the nearest store and tried to find the cheapest, but coolest materials. In the end, I settled on a stack of assorted construction paper, the stuff you might find in a primary school, and started experimenting."

Retracing her own lines with an X-Acto knife, she carves inspiration from organic shapes and phenomena as well as the abstract geometry of fractals, wormholes and MRI scans, layered into 3D sculptures with surprisingly spatial properties.

01

03

**JEN STARK**
01 Candyland
02 Square
03 Afterglow
04 Transfixed

04

JEN STARK
Burst

01

02

03

**JEN STARK**
01 Paper Anomaly
02 Burst (detail)
03 Piece of an Infinite Whole
*Installed in a gallery wall.*

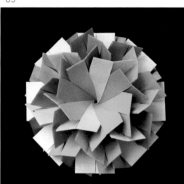

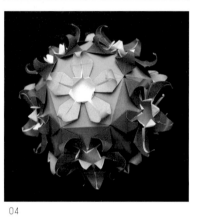

**MEENAKSHI MUKERJI**

01 <u>QRSTUVWXYZ Stars</u>
   *Made with 90 square pieces of
   paper, using no cuts or glue.*

02 <u>Flowered Sonobe & Icosahedron
   with Waves</u>
   *Both models are made up of 30
   units each starting with rectangles.*

03 <u>RSTUVWXYZ Rectangles</u>
   *Made with 72 1x2 rectangles.*

04 <u>Flowered Dodecahedron</u>

**MATTHEW SHLIAN**
05 <u>Warped Stellation</u>

## RICHARD SWEENEY

06 <u>Icosahedron</u>
07 <u>Icosahedron II</u>
08 <u>Tetrahedron</u>

*Any form imaginable can be rendered through drawing, but when modelling in paper, an object has to be physically shaped. When faced with a flat sheet of material, there is no obvious indication of how it can be manipulated into a three dimensional object. The limitations of paper as a form-making material offer a challenge, which through playful investigation results in tangible models. Physical models provide a better indication of proportion and construction than drawings alone, bringing material to the forefront of the design process.*

09 <u>Beauty</u>

*Photograph for the Strategic Hotel annual report developed in collaboration with the Chicago-based graphic design company Samata Mason.*

06

07

09

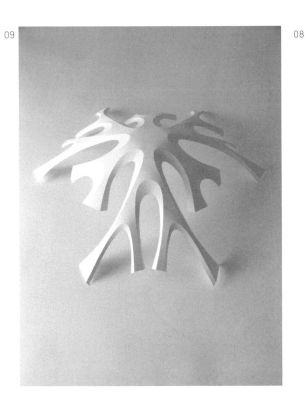

08

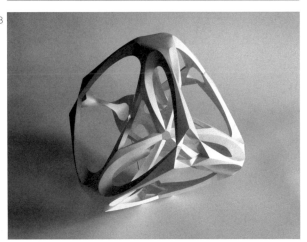

**ANDREA RUSSO**
01 Cogitatio I
02 Radial I
03 Dome
04 Stalagmites tessellation
05 Apiarium ( Lamp )- XIV VII MMVIII
06 Flamma Crispata
*All made from one uncut sheet of paper.*

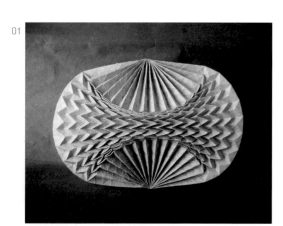

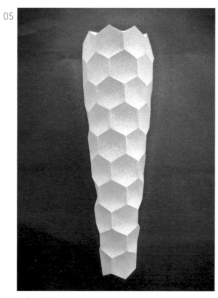

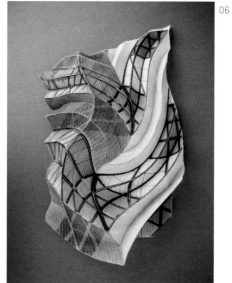

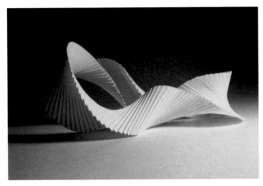

**RICHARD SWEENEY**
07 <u>Untitled</u>
08 <u>Untitled (maquette)</u>
*Paper folded into a vast number
of shapes and structures by only
slightly varying the folding template.
Initially the layouts were drawn
by hand, but by translating these
to Autocad, the working process
became much more streamlined
– the physical models informing
changes to the layout drawing and
vice versa.*

**MATTHEW SHLIAN**
09 <u>C1</u>

**POLLY VERITY**
10 <u>Paper Coral</u>
*Crumpled tissue paper.*

**NORIKO YAMAGUCHI**
01 <u>My Trip in Shanghai</u>
   *Cardboard box made of twisted*
   *Shanghai newspaper*
02 <u>KOSYO (Old Book)</u>

03 **IJM**
   Siba Sahabi
   *Paper objects by Siba Sahabi.*

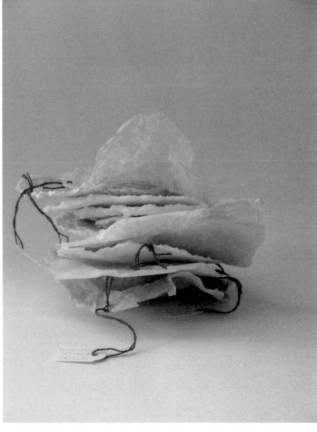

**DESIGNASYL**

**04** <u>Objets en papier</u>
*Sugar-paper pulp, moulded in
textile forms.*

**05** <u>Material experiments</u>
*Material tests with various fibres
and fillers such as bark fibres,
aluminium foil, wood flour, cement,
paste or rubber, sugar, gelatine,
agar-agar, pectin, maize starch,
sugar powder, fructose and salt.*

**FERRY STAVERMAN**
01 Exhibition, Loolaan 49 Gallery
02 Female figure
03 Yellow green tower
04 Yellow fountain
05 Breast
06 Blue fountain

01

02

 03

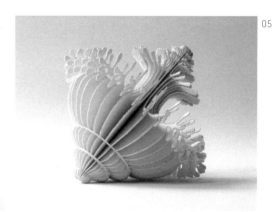 05

 04

 06

### POLLY VERITY

07 Harpy
08 Gryphon
09 Dodo
10 Hippocampus

*Inspired by Tenniel's illustrations for Lewis Carroll's 'Alice's Adventures in Wonderland'.*

07

08

10

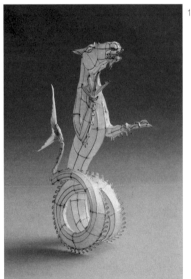

09

RYUJI NAKAMURA
*Kuma*

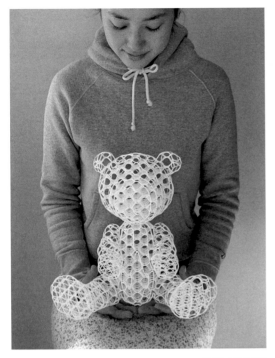

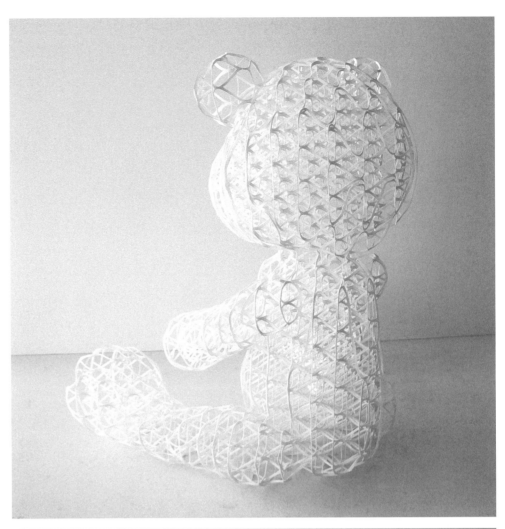

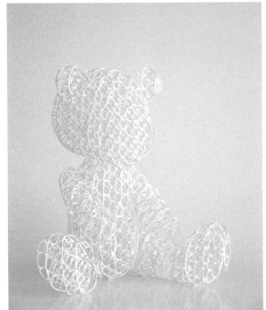

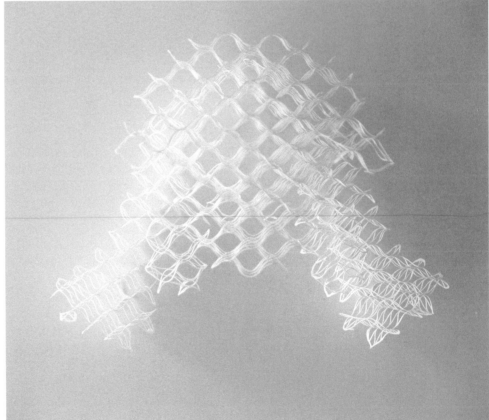

01

02

**LAUREN CLAY**
01 Decked Out In Delight
02 Emptying Marco Polo's Knapsack
03 Little Crumb Bum Keepsake

03

**LAUREN CLAY**

04 <u>Wake Up Dreary Dreamers, I Love You!</u>
05 <u>Lament For The Tragic Love Story of</u>
   <u>Two Parallel Lines</u>
06 <u>Moshi Moshi Anne Truitt Minimini!</u>
07 <u>Big Fat Monochrome With Hangy</u>
   <u>Downy Reflecty Tails</u>

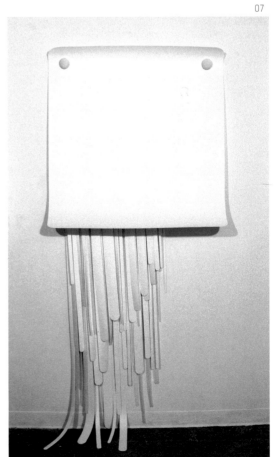

SARAH ILLENBERGER
Fashion Flowers

*right page:*
SARAH ILLENBERGER
Timing

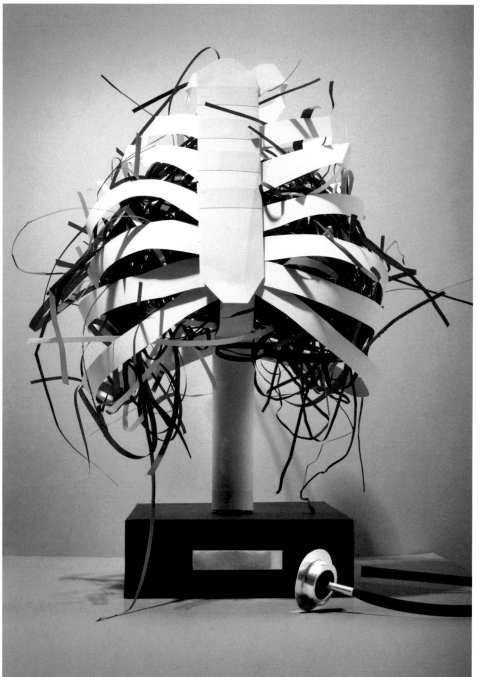

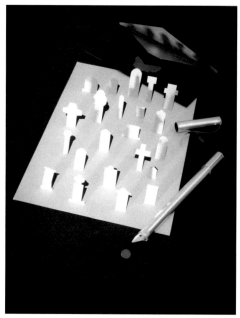

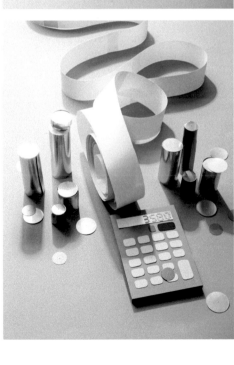

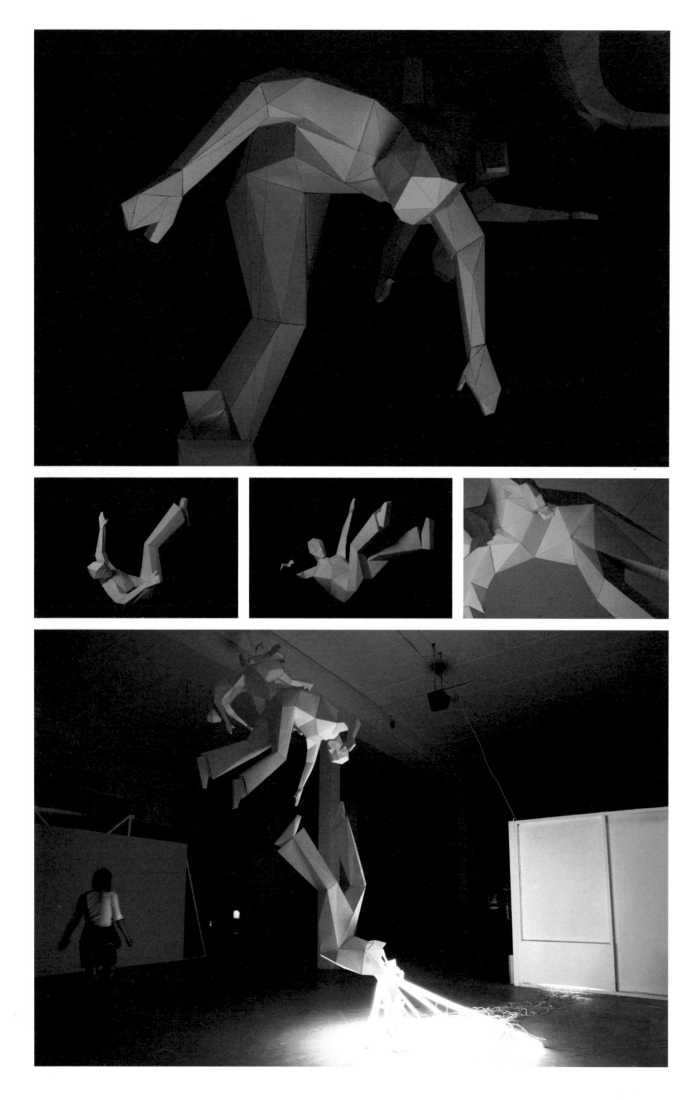

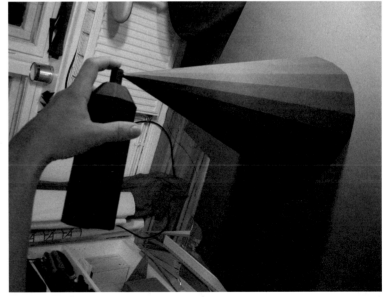

*left page:*

**IVAN TWOHIG**
The FAll
*After the installation was digitally
unfolded, it was printed onto paper
and refolded in the real exhibition
space.*

**JULIEN VALLÉE**
Paper sculpture

### SUSY OLIVEIRA
01 Bird on a log
02 Night eyes open
03 Nothing more, nothing less
04 The only living boy
05 Trap
06 Guts

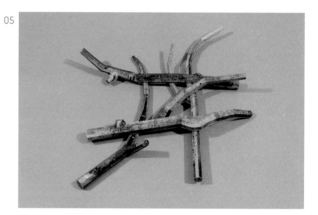

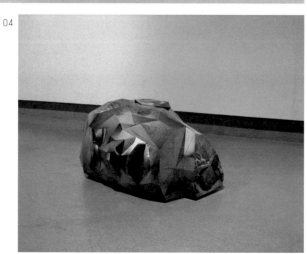

SUSY OLIVEIRA
07 <u>Time is never wasted</u>
08 <u>The Girl and the bear</u>

07

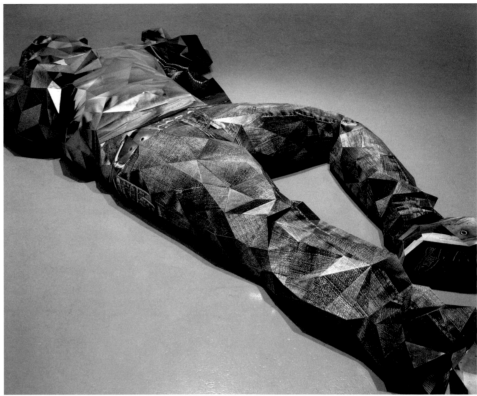

08

# Setting the scene

Lost between data streams and the shifting permutations of our chosen multiple and global identities, we increasingly focus on the realm we inhabit to reassert our sense of self.

Anchored in this physical realm, the following works take the question of identity and belonging that decisive step further – from physical adornments and modification to encompassing, immersive environments that reinvent the world as we know it.

Playing on our sense of scale, from tiny, sheltered microcosms to towering scenarios, the artists assembled in this chapter treat the world as their set. Akin to the parallel worlds hidden in Gregor Schneider's model homes or between the 7th and 8th floor of "Being John Malkovich", they invite us to slip between the cracks and enter their alternate realities, where dreamlike delight meets sinister oppression.

Lulled into a false sense of security by faithful recreations of nostalgic neighbourhoods and idealistic idylls, these Potemkin villages of sheltered environments, of homes that never were, soon give way to more ramified habitats. Here, staggering under their own weight, stacked convolutes like Benjamin van Oost's "Favela" take the model city concept to the brink of collapse. Picking up on this theme of destruction, Adam Klein Hall restages the cataclysmic events of his life in fire, while Swoon's yellowing newsprint creations emphasise their limited lifespan.

In their visual choreography of personal narratives, some appropriate a popular trick from Japanese animation features (think Miyasaki's "Spirited Away") to underscore the difference between deliberately flat and stylised protagonists and a rather more luscious, cinematic backdrop to draw depth and suspense from this striking dichotomy.

At the less figurative end of the scale, artists explore abstract appropriations of space. Some, like Atsushi Fukunaga's self-replicating subtleties, emerge from the creases to colonise their surroundings, or, like Noriko Yamaguchi's delicate, yet hopelessly intertwined paper vines, thrive on organic growth and interaction. Others, like Elrichshausen's paper forests or Mark Fox's proliferating intricacies on the prevalence of apocalyptic themes in major world religions, finally crowd us out of the space we inhabit.

Between the ephemeral lightness of leaves and the solid, lasting sturdiness of a weathered trunk, these works take us back to the roots of all paper – and to our own. Sumer Erek's "Newspaper House" returns recycled newsprint to its former log shape to build a "repository for nationhood, identity and belonging. By creating a house, I not only dwell upon my existence in it, but also build a home for my art."

*right page:*
**THOMAS ALLEN**
Chemistry

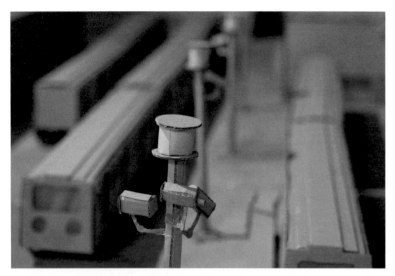

**EDOUARD SAUTAI**
01 <u>209éme arrondissement (nuit)</u>
*During lunchtime over a period
of four weeks, 32 volunters aged
between 11 and 15 were invited to
build their own hut in the class-
room space.*

**HATTIE NEWMAN**
02 <u>The Juniper Tree</u>
*Set built out of recycled cardboard
for a theatre project for Wonderclub
Productions.*

**TOYKYO**
Benjamin Van Oost, Annelies Vercaigne
01 <u>Favela</u>

**TOYKYO**
Bue, Kaiser, Pointdextr & Mr. Fiksit
02 <u>Pillage the village</u>
*Cardboard installation for Expo 2008.*

**ANTOINE+MANUEL**
03 Chapelle
*Scale model for an evolving installation first displayed in an exhibition at Les Arts Décoratifs, Paris.*

**IJM**
**Monique van Bruggen**
04 Late night city life
*Part of an exhibition called 'nachtwandeling'.*

**HATTIE NEWMAN**
05 The Yellow Revolution

03
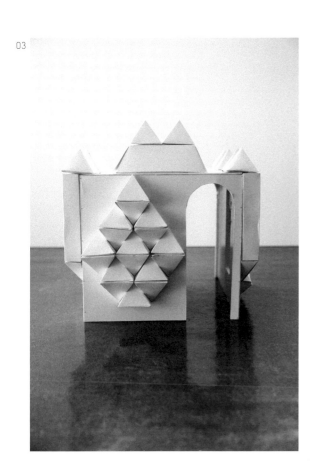

04

05

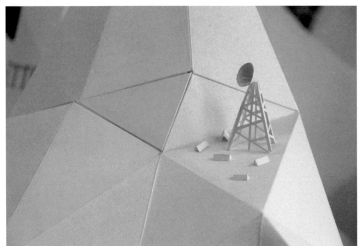

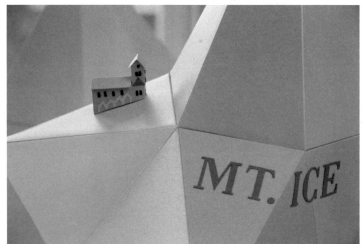

**HATTIE NEWMAN & ALEX OSTROWSKI**
The Fedrigoni Mountains
*Commissioned by Fedrigoni UK.*
*Paper mountain range inspired by*
*the snow-capped Dolomites sur-*
*rounding Fedrigoni's hometown of*
*Verona.*

**FREDRIK ØWESEN**

01 Klein-bottle Bathroom
*Model of a free standing bathroom with a topology identical to a Klein bottle. The shape of the bottle serves as a puzzle. When solved, it imparts new meaning to the room. Freehand polygonal modelling.*

02 Barn at Utsira, Norway
*1:100 scale model folded from a sheet of A3 paper, using techniques from origami tessellations.*

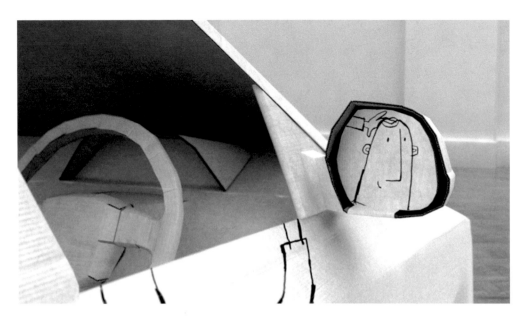

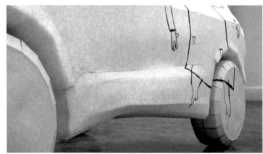

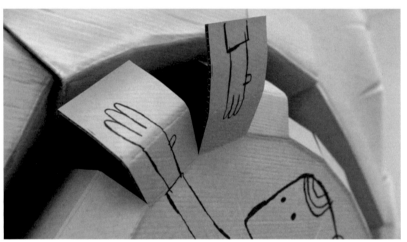

**1ST AVE MACHINE &
PASSION PICTURES**
**Co-directors: Aaron Duffy &
Russell Brooke**
Audi Unboxed spot
*A 1st Ave Machine and Passion
Pictures co-production for BBH.*

*"Unboxing the box," a TV spot for
the Audi Q5, reveals the straightforward ingenuity of technique and
technology with a minimum of twists
and turns.*

*Starting out with the archetype of
pragmatic transportation, the plain
cardboard box, we watch the emer-
gence of a line-drawn character, an in-
quisitive car enthusiast, who starts to
reshape his empty surroundings with
just a few simple strokes and folds.*

*Smoothing out any remaining
bumps, he adds a touch of elegance to
the cardboard lines: all of a sudden,
this most basic of containers has
become a marvel of sleek automotive
engineering.*

完璧を求めて

SIPHO MABONA / MABONA ORIGAMI
In collaboration with
Nordpol+ Hamburg
01 Origami In the Pursuit of Perfection
*Commissioned by Nordpol +*
*Hamburg, Sipho Mabona designed*
*the origami models and consulted*
*the computer animators of this*
*corporate movie that tells the story*
*of Japanese sports brand ASICS.*

CARLO GIOVANI ESTÚDIO
In collaboration with Lobo
02 Akatu Institute
*Stop motion animation for the*
*Akatu Institute for Conscious*
*Consumption, developed*
*by Carlo Giovani Estúdio,*
*produced & directed by Lobo.*

**JESSE BROWN & SEAN PECKNOLD**
Fleet Foxes 'Mykonos'
*Music video for Fleet Foxes song*
*'Mykonos', illustrated & designed by*
*Jesse Brown, animated & directed by*
*Sean Pecknold.*

JULIEN VALLÉE & GUILAUME VALLÉE
UK'S Best bookstores
*For Elle Decoration UK*

**CONTAINERPLUS**

01 <u>Conte de la folie merveilleuse</u>
*Commissioned by talent spotting
agency La Pieuvreto to transform
the boutique hotel Le Placide in
Paris into a land of dark fairy tales.*

02 <u>Playful Type book cover</u>
*Designed for Gestalten's 'Playful
Type – Ephemeral Lettering &
Illustrative Fonts'.*

THOMAS ALLEN
03 Fathom
04 Fancy
05 Explorer, Jackpot, Mate
06 Hindsight
07 Slim
08 Chemistry

04

03

05

06

08

07

## APT & ASYLUM FILMS
### This is Where We Live
Animated short by Apt in
collaboration with Asylum films.

"This is Where We Live", a journey
through the bustling world of literary
highlights, celebrates the 25th anniversary of book publisher Fourth Estate.

A beautiful, sepia-tinted marriage of
stop motion techniques and drawn animation, the short film sees best-selling
tomes spring to life in full retro glory.
With more than 1,000 books thrown

into the mix, we glimpse characters
escaping their own narration to explore
the printed world's wealth of ideas.

A great novella from cover to cover,
the video was pieced together by Apt's
book-loving specialists over the course
of three weeks.

**ILKA HELMIG / LEITWERK**

01 Tristan und Isolde
02 Samson und Dalila
03 Capriccio
   *3D illustration for posters of*
   *Cologne Opera.*

**BEN SCIASCIA**

Svelte 'Grind Your Bones' music video

*Being an unsigned band and having been turned down for video funding, Svelte decided to take matters into their own hands and produced a video using an old digital video camera, a colour printer and a digital stills camera.*

01

**HATTIE NEWMAN**
01 <u>20 Seconds Of Culture</u>
*Animation set for a competition*
*submission through YCN.*

**ANTOINE+MANUEL**
02 <u>Grotto</u>
03 <u>Musical</u>
*Display for a poster and a brochure*
*cover for CNDC – Centre national*
*chorégraphique, Angers.*

02

03

**CONTAINERPLUS**
04 Footwear Fairytales 'Little Red
   Riding Hood'
   *Self initiated project experimenting
   with a paper set created around a
   shoe. One of a series of four, based
   on popular fairytales.*

**TOYKYO**
   Kaiser, Pointdextr, Bue & Mr. Fiksit
05 Eind goed al goed
   *Cardboard installation inside a ship-
   ping container for Expo 2008.*

ILKA HELMIG & KAREL BOONZAAIJER
01 2D Room
*Cardboard installation.*

ANDY MACGREGOR
02 I Love Clocks

03

04

**TAYLOR MCKIMENS**
03 Leak
04 Boob Tube
05 Sorry Truck

05

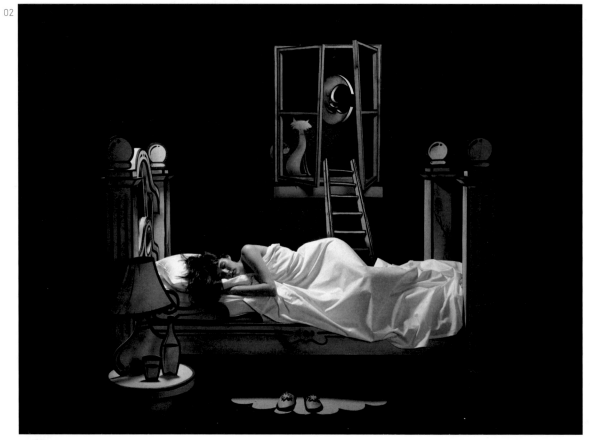

ASIF MIAN / EVAQ STUDIO
01 Kudu 'Back for More'
*Artwork for remix album.*

TOYKYO
Benjamin Van Oost
02 Dormix
SESAMI

*right page*
KIYOSHI KURODA
SESAMI

**CONTAINERPLUS**
TV BAFTAs awards 08
*Sets built for the TV BAFTA awards aftershow party at the Grosvenor Park Hotel, London.*

**CONTAINERPLUS**

<u>Experimental Forest</u>
*Set built for an experimental stop frame animation.*

*Whether hotel interior or awards bash, tabletop trinket or performance piece, containerPLUS treat the world as their set and stage.*

*In their multi-disciplinary concoctions, these mistresses of augmented reality dissect the dichotomy between naïve light and playful dark to rewrite our lives in the crepuscular crevices of fairytale fantasy.*

**JEFF NISHINAKA**
01 Apple Tree
*Paper sculpture installation for the*
*ANA Hotel Tokyo, Japan, to celebrate*
*their 5th anniversary.*

**HATTIE NEWMAN & ALEX OSTROWSKI**
02 YCN LIVE Tree
*Installation made in collaboration*
*with Hackney Borough Council*
*for the evening of the YCN LIVE*
*launch night.*

02

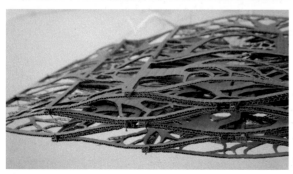

**SWOON**

01 Cut tracing paper
   *Deitch Projects, NYC*
02 Cyclone
03 Miss Rockaway
   *Cut paper and wheatpaste, Kiev*

02

**SWOON**

<u>La Boca del Lobo</u>
*Philedelphia*
<u>Swimming Cities of Switchback
Sea</u>
*Deitch Projects, NYC*
<u>Untitled</u>
<u>Miss Rockaway</u>
*Screenprint and cut paper*
<u>Kiku</u>
*Block print and wheatpaste*
<u>Untitled</u>
*Cut paper and wheatpaste*
<u>Zahra, Swimming Cities of
Switchback Sea</u>
*Deitch Projects, NYC*

03

04

05

## SWOON

01 Portrait of Silvia Elena
02 Lacemaker

Famous for her wheat paste cut-outs plastered across New York City, paper artist Swoon takes a temporary respite from the streets to move her frilly, expressive newsprint creations underground.

Down here, in a basement gallery accessible only through a hole in the floor, she invites us into her netherworld of shadow play and light, of ghosts and rollercoaster rides among the fluttering, ornate figments of her imagination.

Her defining work of death and decay, of tender tragedy, is the Portrait of Silvia Elena, a memorial for an exemplary victim of more than 1,000 unsolved femicides in the Mexican town of Juarez. A defiant visualisation of the crimes' overt cover-up, the portrait draws a metaphorical sheet over the proceedings and serves as a gentle reminder of the ongoing outrage.

01

02

**ATSUSHI FUKUNAGA**
I came to Copenhagen the third times
by Scandlines

**ATSUSHI FUKUNAGA**
01 I came to Copenhagen by Scandlines
02 The sound of growing weed
03 The sound of electric current runs
04 The squeaks of the mice from below
 the floor

07

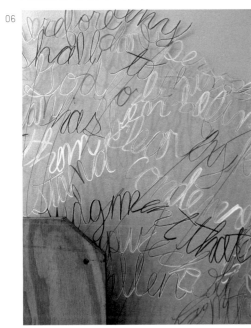

06

**MICHAEL VELLIQUETTE**
The Dark Matters and the Lingering
Lightness
*Installation view at Conduit
Gallery, Dallas.*

01

02

**CHRISTA DONNER**
01 Extrasensory
02 System
*Wall installation with a structure
based on children's pop-up books,
System represents an imaginary
system within the human body,
referencing blood vessels, fallopian
tubes and intestines combined into
a chandelier-like form.*

ILKA HELMIG & KAREL BOONZAAIJER
AND STUDENTS OF THE DESIGN
FACULTY, FH AACHEN
Growing 48 hours
*Design experiment in an aircraft
hangar initiated by Prof. Ilka Helmig
and Prof. Karel Boonzaaijer of FH
Aachen.*

## ADAM KLEIN HALL

01 The City Alight
02 Cut Paper Installation I & II
*The cut paper installations were an exploration of utopian architecture.*

*Expelled from his home by Hurricane Katrina, former New Orleans resident Adam Klein Hall revisits the catastrophe in his art.*

*Harnessing the immense power of natural disasters, of storms, floods and fires, Klein Hall translates the primal intensity of these forces to his techniques. Crinkles, burns and spills bring an element of accident to the creative process and enhance the fragility of his chosen medium.*

*By burning, folding and twirling paper into large-scale organic patterns, he creates dystopian environments that emphasise human impermanence in an era of constant change, yet also allow a sliver of utopia.*

*Carefully singed, yet unconsumed engineering landmarks from different eras survive the elemental assault to offer a jumbled glimpse of a hopeful future that might be ours, after all.*

02

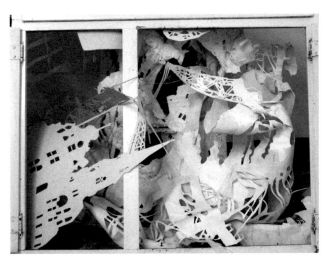

ADAM KLEIN HALL
<u>White Paper Installation</u>
*Large-scale installation made of
burned, folded, and twirled paper.*

MARK FOX
Untitled (Hydra)

02

## NORIKO YAMAGUCHI

01 <u>Growing</u>
02 <u>From Mother</u>
   *Selected work for the Holland Paper
   Biennial 2008 at Museum Rijswijk
   in the Netherlands.*
03 <u>EVOCATIVE</u>
   *Selected work for the Holland Paper
   Biennial 2008 at CODA Apeldoorn in
   the Netherlands.*
04 <u>Foliage</u>
   *Work for the group exhibition 'Fiber
   Biennal' at Snyderman-Works
   Galleries in Philadelphia, USA.*

04

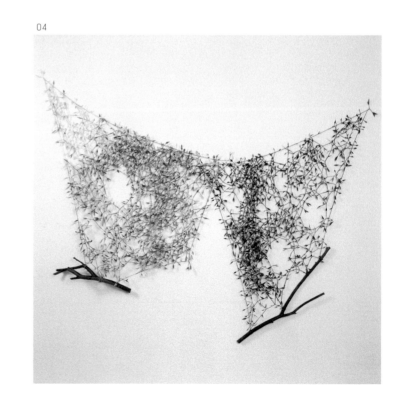

*Noriko Yamaguchi, a graduate of dyeing and weaving, abandoned her two-dimensional textile background for three-dimensional paper concoctions. In the long-winded process of twisting and "knitting" recycled paper, every repetition can spawn a variation, adding chance and complexity to our everyday existence.*

*Sometimes balled up tight and impossibly entangled, sometimes strung out across the room, her twisted strings are twirled from washi*

*(Japanese paper), newsprint or books, thus carrying their own information and stories, albeit indecipherable after the fact.*

*Always working within her surroundings, Yamaguchi spins rhizomes and tales into encompassing installations that interfere with the fabric of space itself.*

## RICHARD SWEENEY

05 <u>Mobius</u>

*A series of sculptural works in paper commissioned by Selfridges for display in the flagship store windows, Orchard Street, London.*

06 <u>Beta Sheet</u>

*Site-specific commission produced for the Stamp Staircase at Somerset House, London. Beta Sheet comprises twenty six unique, hand-pleated sections, glued together to create a continuous sheet. The pleat pattern was derived from a combination of computer-generated models and hand-made test pieces.*

05

06

NONDESIGNS
Scott Franklin & Miao Miao
Living Paper (Exhibit Space)
*Conceived as an exhibition space to house NONdesigns' first set of prototypes including the WET lamp, TOPO table and MONO lounge. The environment responds to the visitors as if it were a living organism. Glowing touch sensors throughout the space caused the honeycomb to expand and contract, changing the light qualities, and size and shape of the interior.*

**MOLO**

01 <u>Softhousing</u>

02 <u>Folded and opened 6' tall textile</u>
   <u>softwalls</u>
   *A honeycomb geometry is applied to*
   *simple lightweight sheets of humble*
   *materials of paper and non-woven*
   *textiles. The honeycomb geometry,*
   *lends these structures high strength*
   *and flexible resilience.*

03 <u>Softseating</u>
   *Belongs to molo's family of expand-*
   *able and compressible honeycomb*
   *structures.*

03

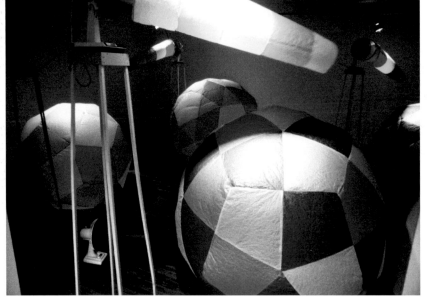

EDOUARD SAUTAI
Ballons et manches à air
*Sewed silk paper; exhibition at*
*Clark Galery, Montréal.*

EDOUARD SAUTAI
Home sweet home
*Exhibition at the university museum, Chiang Maï.*

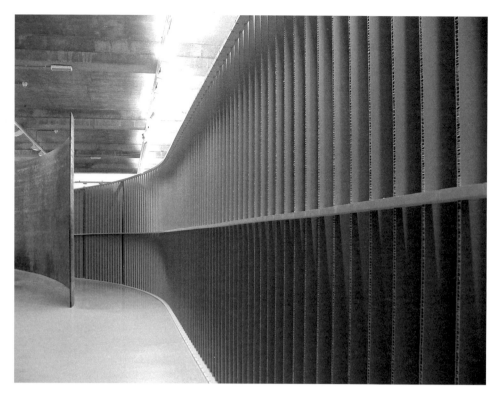

**STEALTH.UNLIMITED**
Ana Dzokic, Marc Neelen &
Mario Campanella
<u>Cut for Purpose</u>

01 *Cut for Purpose – starting condition*

*artists featured:*
02 **Strange Attractors**
03 **Cucosa artists collective**
04 **Robbert de Vrieze**

*Carve your own niche!*

*Challenging the concept of space itself – and the role of an exhibiting gallery, Cut for Purpose relies on individual breakthroughs for access to art.*

*After filling a 600 square metre space at the Rotterdam-based Museum Boijmans van Beuningen with a tight honeycomb structure of man-sized cardboard sheets, external collaborators were invited to open up their own territories, to tap into this creative mine and appropriate the unhewn behemoth.*

*Negotiating this tricky task, the participants started to tackle the temporary inversion of space and shape their cardboard surroundings. Slowly, over the course of two months, the previously impenetrable gallery became a creative hive that betrayed the temporal progress, tracks and explorative efforts of its individual members in a three-dimensional imprint and echo of their collective dialogue.*

03

04

CARL KLEINER
01 Ceremony #2

DONNIE LUU
02 Potential Space
*Made of over 200 feet of paper,
the piece was installed in the
hallway space at main EDA of the
Design/Media Arts department at
the University of California,
Los Angeles (UCLA).*

02

**PEZO VON ELLRICHSHAUSEN**
Forestal

*This forest-like installation by Mauricio Pezo and Sofía von Ellrichshausen consists of fifty-five columns made from crumpled pieces of paper.*

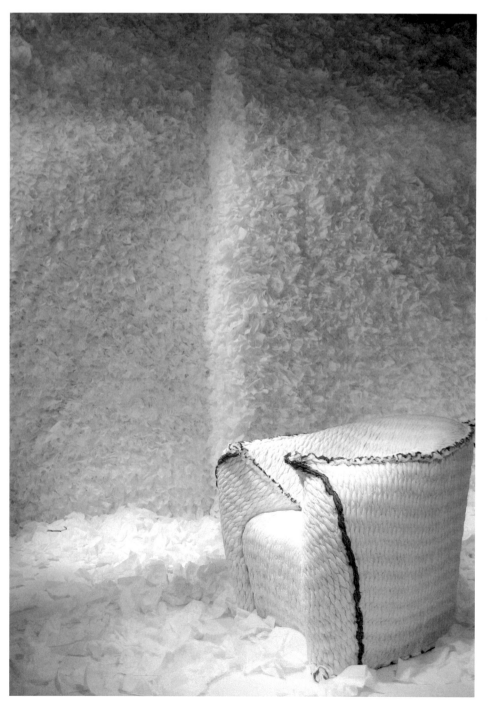

**TOKUJIN YOSHIOKA**
Moroso NY
*Entire space covered with approximately 30,000 sheets of tissue at Moroso showroom in New York.*

**ADRIAN MERZ & CORNELIA HESS**
Il était une fois… Winter 1972

American perfumer Christopher Brosius aims to capture, preserve and transform specific memories, stories and situations into sensual olfactory experiences.

One of his signature scents, depicted in this installation, takes us back to the winter of 1972, to untouched snow, frost-covered earth and the perfumer's own particular memories.

For the accompanying poster campaign, Merz and Hess translate the scent-from-memory into a stark visual statement: thousands of pristine white post-it notes cover a living room to create a deceptively fluffy – and cosy – winter wonderland.

**JOHAN HJERPE**
Happy Room
*Installation as part of*
*DOTDOTDOTDOT, a group exhibition*
*in homage to Yayoi Kusama.*

**SHAZ MADANI**
01 D&G Window installation
*Window installation for estate*
*agents Douglas and Gordon in South*
*Kensington.*

**ATSUSHI FUKUNAGA**
02 Schmetterling

**ELINA MINN & ANNA VIRTANEN**

01  B-butik
*Paper installation in the back
room of B-galleria.*

02  Kokoro & Moi
*Paper installation for
Kokoro & Moi studio.*

03  Artnet
*Paper installation for the attic
of Artprint print house.*

*right page:*
Paper installation for Trendi
*Paper installation for a fashion
editorial in Trendi magazine.*

PETER CALLESEN
Mirage
*Mirrored staircase installation at*
*Gallery Koch und Kesslau, Berlin.*

## SUMER EREK
Newspaper House

With free sheets thriving despite the plight of the newspaper industry, plenty of papers end up in the street, on bus seats or café floors. An exercise in communal recycling, Cyprus-born conceptual artist Sumer Erek and his collaborators turned 120,000 free papers into building blocks for a 12-foot house in both London and Liverpool. Rolled up into log shapes, the raw material returns to its natural state and becomes part of Erek's recycled "log cabin".

Expanding on the notion of the house as a home and metaphor for identity and belonging, the resulting 'Newspaper House' doubles as a shelter, workshop and – finally – finished art and gallery space. Erected over a period of two months together with local artists, residents, visitors, community organisations and schools, the shared communal experience raises awareness on environmental issues and urban waste.

# Index

**1ST AVE MACHINE & PASSION PICTURES**
USA | www.1stavemachine.com |
United Kingdom | www.passion-pictures.com |
Audi Unboxed spot: Client: Audi |
Agency: BBH | Creative Directors: Nick
Kidney [m1], Kevin Stark | Creatives: Maja
Fernquist, Joakim Saul | Music: 'The Car Song' Woody
Guthrie | Production Company: Co-produced
by Passion Pictures + 1st Ave Machine |
Co-directors: Aaron Duffy (1st Ave) and
Russell Brooke (Passion) | Producer: Belinda
Blacklock, Anna Lord | Executive Producers:
Michael Adamo (Passion) and Serge Patzak
(1st Ave) | Animation: Passion Pictures
page 192 | VIDEO-DVD

**A4ADESIGN**
Italy | www.a4adesign.it
Photo (right image) by Vera Cannone
page 56

**ADAM KLEIN HALL**
USA | www.adamkhall.com
page 225 | The City Alight: Photo by
Jennifer Mansfield
page 226, 227: Photos by Jennifer Mansfield
pages 225, 226, 227

**ADRIAN MERZ & CORNELIA HESS**
Switzerland | www.i-never-kissed-a-dog.ch |
www.frauhess.ch
page 241

**AKATRE**
France | www.akatre.com
pages 110, 111, 113, 114, 115

**AKS / KWAN THUNG SENG**
Malaysia | www.aksfile.blogspot.com
page 76

**AMY CARTWRIGHT**
USA | www.amycartwright.com
page 77

**ANDREA RUSSO**
Italy | www.andreaorigami.altervista.org
pages 58, 166

**ANDY MACGREGOR**
United Kingdom | www.andymacgregor.com
page 59: Photo by Adam Laycock
page 206: Photos by Jasper White
pages 59, 206

**ANGELLO GARCÍA BASSI / CUBOTOY**
Chile | www.cubotoy.co.nr
page 83 | DVD-ROM

**ANTOINE+MANUEL**
France | www.antoineetmanuel.com
pages 14, 15, 42, 189, 204

**APT & ASYLUM FILMS**
United Kingdom | www.aptstudio.com |
www.asylumfilms.co.uk
This is Where We Live:
Directors: Ben Falk & Josiah Newbolt |
Executive Producers: Peter Collingridge
& James Bridle | Producer: Phil Vanier |
Production Designer: Philippa Culpepper
| Animation Director: Jordan Wood |
Supervising Animator: Mickey Bignell |
Composer: Mike Chalmers
pages 198 - 201 | VIDEO-DVD

**ASIF MIAN / EVAQ**
USA | www.evaq.com
page 148 | Aesop Rock 'Fast Cars':
Director: Asif Mian | DP: Valentina
Caniglia | Art Director: Asif Mian |
Producer: Chesley Heymsfield | Post
Production: Evaq Studio |
Music: Aesop Rock
page 208: Art Director: Asif Mian |
Photo by Zak Mulligan
pages 148, 208 | VIDEO-DVD

**ATSUSHI FUKUNAGA**
Japan | www.atsushifukunaga.jpn.org
pages 219, 220, 243

**BELA BORSODI**
USA | www.belaborsodi.com
pages 95 - 97

**BEN SCIASCIA**
New Zealand | www.sciascia.co.nz
Svelte 'Grind Your Bones' music video:
Photographers & Set Builders:
Ben Sciascia, Tim Stewart and Jamie
Woolright (the band) | Additional Frame
Cutters: Christina Rhodes, Dominic
Corry, Muray Bean, Renee Woolright &
Travis Woolright | Music: Svelte
page 203 | VIDEO-DVD

**BENT IMAGE LAB**
USA | www.bentimagelab.com
They Might Be Giants 'I'm Impressed':
Production Company: Bent Image Lab |
Director/Designer: Rob Shaw | Executive
Producers: Ray Di Carlo, Chel White
| Senior Producer: Tsui Ling Toomer |
Producer: Kara Place | Bent Creative
Partner: Chel White | Directors of
Photography: Mark Eifert, James Birkett
| Animators: Rob Shaw, Sarah Hulin |
Assistant Animators: Brian Kinkley,
Marty Easterday | Character Designer:
Bartek Prusiewicz | Storyboard Artist:
Monique Ligons | Art Department Director:
Solomon Burbridge | Art Department:
Diana Joy Parker, Marty Easterday |
Paper Artists: Javan Ivey, Alisa Stern,
Jamie Edwards, Jesse Hollis, Kimi
Kapowitz | Post-production Supervisor:
Orland Nutt | Digital Compositors: Brian
Kinkley, Orland Nutt | Online Editor: Jon
Weigand | Music: They Might Be Giants
page 91 | VIDEO-DVD

**BOMBO!**
Italy | www.bomboland.com
page 43

**BOSQUE**
Argentina | www.holabosque.com.ar
pages 14, 44

**BOVEY LEE**
USA | www.boveylee.com
pages 130 - 133

**BRAINSTRIKERS ARTDENKA**
Japan | www.artdenka.com
page 77

**BRIAN CASTLEFORTE**
USA | www.castleforte.com |
www.nicebunny.com
pages 78, 82

**BRIAN DETTMER**
USA | www.briandettmer.com
World Science | Complete Book of Ballets |
New Books of Knowledge | Full Set of
Funk: Images courtesy of the Artist
and Packer Schopf | Modern Progress |
Pattern Layouts | New Universal: Images
courtesy of the artist and MiTO Gallery |
The Connoisseur's Complete Guide |
Mound 2 | Webster Two Point Oh |
Prevent Horizon: Images courtesy of
the Artist and Kinz + Tillou Fine Art
pages 156 - 159 | VIDEO-DVD

**BRIAN GUBICZA**
USA | www.goobeetsa.com
page 76 | DVD-ROM

**BROCK DAVIS STUDIO: LASER BREAD**
USA | www.itistheworldthatmadeyousmall.com
pages 9, 14

**CARA BARER**
USA | www.carabarer.com
page 155

**CARL KLEINER**
Sweden | www.carlkleiner.com
pages 108, 210, 238

**CARLO GIOVANI ESTÚDIO**
Brazil | www.carlogiovani.com
page 41 | TIM Tales: Illustration, Sets
and Stop Motion: Carlo Giovani Estúdio
(Carlo Giovani, Heitor Yida, Fabiano
Silva, Sheila Hirata, Lucia Farias and
Pedro Hamdan) & Everson Nazari (dslab)
| Direction, Editing and Post Production:
AD Studio | Agency: Lew'Lara
page 70 | Havaianas Kids: Photos by
Fernando Nalon | Agency: Almap BBDO
pages 88, 89 | Mundos Invisíveis:
Photography: Carlo Giovani | Animation:
Carlo Giovani, Rodrigo Silveira, Ligia Jeon
page 90 | Elma Chips Kids:
Illustration, Sets and Stop Motion:
Carlo Giovani Estúdio (Carlo Giovani &
Bruno Algarve) | Direction, Editing and
Post Production: AD Studio | Agency:
Almap | Photography: Digão
page 91 | Gordo Freak Show:
Illustration, sets and stop motion:
Carlo Giovani Estúdio (Carlo Giovani &
Bruno Algarve) | Direction, Editing and
Post Production: MTV Brasil
(Ana Starling and Macau Amarau)
page 193 | Akatu Institute:
Art and animation: Carlo Giovani
Estúdio (Carlo Giovani, Bruno Algarve,
Ligia Jeon & Rodrigo Silveira) & Lobo |
Producer: Lobo | Photography:
Marcio Simnch | Agency: Leo Burnett
pages 41, 70, 88, 89, 90, 91, 92, 93, 193 |
VIDEO-DVD

**CHRIS HEADS**
Italy | www.chrisheads.com
Stylist: Peter Breen
page 105

**CHRISTA DONNER**
USA | www.christadonner.com
page 223

**CHRISTIAN TAGLIAVINI**
Switzerland | www.christiantagliavini.com
page 104

**CHRISTOPHER BONNETTE**
USA | www.macula.tv
Squealers: Photos by Joseph Bartlett
page 79 | DVD-ROM

**CIARA PHELAN**
United Kingdom | www.iamciara.co.uk
page 22 | Open Days: In collaboration
with Tom Rowe & Adam Ellison
page 44 | Little Red: By Ciara Phelan
pages 22, 26, 44 | VIDEO-DVD

**COLETTE FU**
USA | www.fusansan.com
Created while artist in residence at
Provincetown Fine Arts Work Center,
Massachusetts & Robert M Macnamara
Foundation, Maine (Rodin Museum)
page 147

**CONTAINERPLUS**
United Kingdom | www.containerplus.co.uk
pages 14, 117, 196, 205, 211, 212

**CORD WOYWODT / FALTPLATTE**
Germany | www.faltplatte.de
Photos by Stephan Falk
page 63

**CRAIG KIRK**
United Kingdom | www.craigkirk.net
page 62

**DAN MCPHARLIN**
Australia | www.danmcpharlin.com
*Moog Acid*: Project Art Direction by
Non-Format
page 60

**DESIGNASYL**
Switzerland | www.designasyl.blog.ch
page 169

**DIRK BEHLAU**
Germany | www.pixeleye.de
Designed by Christian Schaarschmidt
(www.illunatic.de) | Produced by Dirk
Behlau | Photos by Dirk Behlau
page 82 | DVD-ROM

**DONNIE LUU**
USA | www.donnieluu.com
pages 109, 238

**EDOUARD SAUTAI**
France | www.edouardsautai.com
*page 187 | 209ème arrondissement (nuit)*:
Edouard Sautai | Photography on
aluminium 98 x 120
pages 187, 234, 235

**ELINA MINN & ANNA VIRTANEN**
Finland | www.tuhru.net
*page 245*: Photo by Elina Simonen
pages 244 - 245

**ELISABETH LECOURT**
United Kingdom | www.elisabethlecourt.com
pages 98, 99

**ELOOLE**
Spain | www.eloole.com
page 68 | DVD-ROM

**EVE DUHAMEL**
Canada | www.eveduhamel.com
pages 21, 44

**EVELINA BRATELL**
Sweden | www.evelinabratell.com
pages 102, 103

**FERRY STAVERMAN**
Netherlands | www.ferrystaverman.nl
*Breast*: Courtesy J. van der Graaf |
*Female figure*: Courtesy R. van Heuven
– van Nes
page 170

**FREDRIK ØWESEN**
Norway | www.flickr.com/photos/owesen/
*Barn at Utsira, Norway*: Photo by
Feileacán McCormick
page 191

**FULGURO**
Switzerland | www.fulguro.ch
In Collaboration with Axel Jaccard
page 59

**FUPETE**
Italy | www.fupete.com
First event of Urban Portraits series –
Curatorial Fabio Campagna
page 72

**FWIS**
USA | www.fwis.com
Readymech Cameras at Corbis:
www.corbis.readymech.com
page 71 | DVD-ROM

**GHOST ROBOT**
USA | www.ghostrobot.com
*Bonnaroo Lineup Announcement 2009*:
Director: Elliot Jokelson | Producer:
Matthew Achterberg | Exec. Producers:
Mark De Pace, Zach Mortensen |
Art Director: Andrew Hamilton | Lead
Animator: Jasmina Mathieu | Assistant
Animators: Mike Healy, Kelly Goeller |
Music: Michael Saltzman | Sound Design:
Robin Shore | Color Correction: Jerome
Thelia | Paper Printing: B Squared |
Production Coordinator: Stine Moisen |
Sterographic Assistant: Trevor Tweeton |
Stereographic Consultant: Greg Dinkins |
Paper Consultants: Angel Thompson-
Georges, Steve Varvaro | Rig Fabricator:
Ryan Cheresnick | Production Assistant:
Alice Millar | Fabrication Interns: Nadirah
Zakariya, Emma Beebe, Natalia Molina,
Katie Love, Zachariah Durr, Emily Searle,
Judge Finklea Hang Xu, Lena Hawkins,
Brenda Malivini, Basil Whatley, Laila Lot,
Joy Sunjooft, Bracey Smith, Emma Mead,
Crystal Farshchi, Dan Olavarria, Chrystie
Cole, Tierney Cole, Lisette Johnson
page 27 | VIDEO-DVD

**HATTIE NEWMAN**
United Kingdom |
www.hattienewman.blogspot.com
*page 61*: In collaboration with Rude
*pages 190, 213*: In collaboration with
Alex Ostrowski | www.alexostrowski.com
pages 45, 61, 149, 187, 189, 190, 204, 213

**HELEN FRIEL**
United Kingdom | www.helenfriel.co.uk
pages 32, 33, 39

**HELEN MUSSELWHITE**
United Kingdom | www.helenmusselwhite.com
page 46

**HINA AOYAMA**
France | www.hinaaoyama.com
*page 129 | Lettre de Voltaire*: Photo by
Ohguri Megumi
pages 128, 129

**HORRORWOOD**
Japan | www.horrorwood.info
page 86 | DVD-ROM

**IAN WRIGHT**
USA | www.mrianwright.co.uk
Commissioned by Art Director
Greg Burke for Atlantic Records NYC
page 30

**IJM**
Netherlands | www.ijm.nl
*page 168*: Photos by Anne Dokter |
Paper Objects: Siba Sahabi | Styling:
Frank Visser
*page 189 | Late night city life*:
Monique van Bruggen for IJM | Credits:
Karin Nussbaumer/Frank Visser
pages 118 - 121, 168, 189

**ILKA HELMIG / LEITWERK**
Germany | www.ilkahelmig.de |
www.leitwerk.com
*page 202*: Project management:
Oliver Culmsee / Ramona Sekula
*page 206*: In collaboration with
Karel Boonzaaijer | Exhibition
Organisation: Leitwerk
*page 224*: In collaboration with Karel
Boonzaaijer and students of the Design
Faculty, FH Aachen | Photos by Ilka Helmig
(upper images), Sören Helbig (lower image)
pages 202, 206, 224

**INGRID SILIAKUS**
Netherlands | www.ingrid-siliakus.exto.org
pages 144, 145

**IVAN RICCI**
Italy | www.kawaii-style.net
page 77 | DVD-ROM

**IVAN TWOHIG**
Ireland | www.ivantwohig.com
page 180

**JACQUELINE RUSH LEE**
USA | www.jacquelinerushlee.com
*page 153 | Stack*: Photo by Jacqueline
Rush Lee, Hawaii, *Book of R's | Cube*:
Photos by Paul Kodama, Hawaii
*page 154 | Devotion Series*: Photos by
Paul Kodama, Hawaii | In the Collection
of Dean Geleynse, Hawaii ('*Unfurled*') |
In the Collection of Elizabeth Grossman,
Hawaii ('*Unfurled II*') | *Ex Libris*: Photos by
Brad Goda, Hawaii | In the Collection of the
Contemporary Museum, Honolulu, Hawaii
pages 153, 154

**JASON HARLAN**
USA | www.harlancore.com
Photos by Vin Breau
pages 80, 81 | DVD-ROM

**JAVAN IVEY**
USA | www.javanivey.com
*page 26 | My Paper Mind*: By Javan Ivey
page 26 | VIDEO-DVD

**JEAN JULLIEN**
United Kingdom | www.jeanjullien.com
pages 18, 40

**JEFF NISHINAKA**
USA | www.papercutstudio.net
*pages 134, 135*: Photos by Ed Ikuta
*page 213*: Art Director: Mari Makinami/
International Design Association,
Tokyo Japan
pages 134, 135, 213

**JENNY GRIGG**
Australia | www.jennygrigg.com
*page 36*: Peter Carey's backlist published by Random House Australia.
*pages 34, 35*: Commissioned by Danish
publishers Lindhardt og Ringhof
pages 34 - 36

**JEN STARK**
USA | www.jenstark.com
*pages 160, 161*: Photos by Jen Stark and
Harlan Erskine (*Square | Afterglow*)
*pages 162, 163, 256*: Photos by Harlan
Erskine
pages 160 - 163, 256

**JEREMIAS BÖTTCHER**
Germany | www.studiobrigant.com
*page 110 | Papstars*:
Production: Studiobrigant | Director:
Jeremias Böttcher | Camera: Thomas
Naumann | Music: Jazalou and
Lockefella | Costumes & Decorations:
Jeremias Böttcher | Post Production:
Florian Feldmann
*page 186*: Photo by Uros Djurovic
pages 110, 186 | VIDEO-DVD

**JESSE BROWN & SEAN PECKNOLD**
USA | www.paperspencil.com |
www.bygrandchildren.com
*Fleet Foxes 'Mykonos'*:
Artist/Illustrator: Jesse Brown |
Director/Animator: Sean Pecknold |
Animation Assistants: Toby Liebowitz
& Chris Ando | Art Director: Sean
Pecknold | Produced by Grandchildren |
Labels: Bella Union & Sub Pop |
Music: Fleet Foxes
page 194 | VIDEO-DVD

# Index

**JULIEN VALLÉE**
Canada | www.jvallee.com
page 20: Art Direction: Julien Vallée
& Dixon Baxi | Design: Julien Vallée |
Photographer: Simon Duhamel |
Special thanks: Eve Duhamel
page 21 | Tangible – High-Touch Visuals:
Photographer: Simon Duhamel | Special
thanks: Eve Duhamel, Matthias Hubner |
Raking leaves in the wind: In collabora-
tion with Eve Duhamel & Brent Wadden
page 148 | Black & White teaser:
In collaboration with BleuBlancRouge |
Music: René-Pierre Guérin
page 195: In collaboration with
Guilaume Vallée | Photos by
Simon Duhamel
pages 20, 21, 148, 181, 195 | VIDEO-DVD

**JOHAN HJERPE**
Sweden | www.johanhjerpe.com
page 242

**JUNGMO KWON**
South Korea | www.jungmokwon.blogspot.com
page 214

**KEETRA DEAN DIXON**
USA | www.fromkeetra.com
pages 16, 17, 108

**KENN MUNK**
Denmark | www.kennmunk.com
page 66 | Yoyoyo Acapulco Antlor:
Client: Yoyoyo Acapulco
pages 66 - 67 | DVD-ROM

**KERSTIN ZU PAN**
Germany | www.zu-pan.com
Photography: Kerstin zu Pan |
Wig: Acacio da Silva | Make-up Artist:
Karla Neff | Installation: Yuka Oyama |
Models: Le Jacques Helene/Constanze/
Laust@Viva
pages 122 - 125

**KIYOSHI KURODA**
Japan | www.kiyoshikuroda.jp
page 209: Client: Asahi Shimbun
Publications Inc. | Photo by Akira
Kitajima (SPUTNIK) | Hair & Make-up:
Fusae Tachibana | Stylist: Miki Aizawa
page 116: Photo by Emiko Morizaki
(Super Sonic) | Make-up: Izumi Okada |
Model: Reika Hashimoto (Rhythmedia inc.)
| Clothes: Rie Hirota
pages 116, 209

**KOUICHI OKAMOTO / KYOUEI DESIGN**
Japan | www.kyouei-ltd.co.jp
Credits: Kyouei design
page 57

**LAUREN CLAY**
USA | www.doublefluff.com
pages 174, 175 | Emptying Marco Polo's
Knapsack: Image Courtesy of Larissa
Goldston Gallery | Wake Up Dreary
Dreamers | I Love You!: Images Courtesy
of Larissa Goldston Gallery
pages 174, 175

**LISA OCCHIPINTI**
USA | www.locchipinti.com
page 153

**LOBO**
Brazil | www.lobo.cx
Capitu: Creative Direction:
Mateus de Paula Santos & Carlos Bêla |
Concept: Carlos Bêla, Roger Marmo,
Mateus de Paula Santos | Design &
Animation: Carlos Bêla | Assistant
Animator: Rachel Moraes | Production:
João Tenório | Music: Tim Rescala
pages 28, 29 | VIDEO-DVD

**LOCOGRAFIX - PLAYROLL**
Netherlands | www.locografix.com
page 82 | DVD-ROM

**LUCYANDBART**
Netherlands | www.lucyandbart.com
Credits: Lucy McRae and Bart Hess
page 112

**MACOTO SAITO**
Japan | www.macoto-s.net
page 106

**MARK FOX**
USA | www.larissagoldston.com/artists/
markfox/index.aspx
page 221: Photo Courtesy Larissa
Goldston Gallery
pages 228, 229: Installation at the Santa
Barbara Contemporary Arts Forum
pages 221, 228, 229

**MARK JAMES**
United Kingdom | www.markjamesworks.com
pages 74, 75, 76 | DVD-ROM

**MARKO ZUBAK**
Croatia | www.markozubak.com |
www.yebomaycu.com
page 86

**MARSHALL ALEXANDER**
Netherlands | www.marshallalexander.net
page 69 | DVD-ROM

**MATT HAWKINS**
USA | www.custompapertoys.com
page 79

**MATTHEW SHLIAN**
USA | www.mattshlian.com
pages 76, 164, 167

**MEENAKSHI MUKERJI**
USA | www.origamee.net
page 164

**MEMORANDOM**
United Kingdom | www.memo-random.com
page 25

**MICHAEL VELLIQUETTE**
USA | www.velliquette.com
page 46: Courtesy of the Artist. Private
collection, San Antonio, TX
page 47-49 | Tower of Power | Borders
Beyond | Snuggie | Happy Minotaur |
El Profesor | Hypno, Humbaba |
Hypnotic Serpent of the Unconscious
Lair: Courtesy of the Artist and DCKT
Contemporary, NY | Familiar | Doom Day
Afternoon: Courtesy of the Artist and
DCKT Contemporary, NY. Private col-
lection, NY | The Observer Summoned:
Courtesy of the Artist. Private collec-
tion, Kerrville, TX | The Grand Showman
Reborn: Courtesy of the Artist and
DCKT Contemporary, NY. Private
collection, Chicago
page 222: Courtesy the artist
pages 46 - 49, 222

**MOLO**
Canada | www.molodesign.com
page 233

**NANIBIRD**
Japan | www.nanibird.com
The Dears: In collaboration with
Ben the Illustrator
page 77

**NICOLA FROM BERN**
Switzerland | www.nicolafrombern.com |
www.foldschool.com
Photos by Rolf Küng (www.kuengfu.ch)
page 56 | DVD-ROM

**NIESSEN & DE VRIES**
Netherlands | www.niessendevries.nl
page 16

**NONDESIGNS**
USA | www.nondesigns.com
page 232

**NORIKO YAMAGUCHI**
Japan | www.norikoyamaguchi.com
page 168: Photos by Hideto Nagatsuka
page 230 | Growing | Foliage: Photos by
Hideto Nagatsuka
pages 168, 230

**ODED EZER**
Israel | www.odedezer.com
Credits: © Oded Ezer Typography |
Photos by Oded Ezer
page 10 | I ♥ Milton: Photos by Idan Gil
page 12 | CoPro2000: Photos by
Amos Rafaeli
pages 10 - 12, 17

**OLOF BRUCE, TOM ERIKSSON &
LIV WADSTRÖM**
Sweden | www.olofbruce.se |
www.tomeriksson.se | www.livwadstrom.se
page 146

**OWEN GILDERSLEEVE**
United Kingdom | www.eveningtweed.com
pages 13, 38

**PAPER FOLDABLES**
USA | www.paperfoldables.com
Giant Street Fighter Paper Foldables:
Photo by Alex J. Berliner (c) Berliner
Studio/BEImages
page 72 | DVD-ROM

**PERRO LOCO**
Spain |
www.flickr.com/photos/fragile_freak/
page 73

**PETER CALLESEN**
Denmark | www.petercallesen.com
page 138: Photo (upper image) by
Anders Sune Berg
page 140: Photos by Mette Bersang
pages 127, 136 - 141, 246, 247

**PETER LUNDGREN**
Sweden | www.peterlundgren.se
page 61

**PEZO VON ELLRICHSHAUSEN**
Chile | www.pezo.cl
page 239

**PIERRE VANNI**
France | www.pierrevanni.com
page 24 | Les Siestes electroniques:
With the help of Thomas Dudon
pages 23, 24

**PIXELGARTEN**
Germany | www.pixelgarten.de
page 22: Client: NEON Magazin |
Photographers: Markus Burke &
Roderick Aichinger Produktion | Art
Direction: Jonas Natterer | Set Design:
Pixelgarten | Styling: Maike Rohlfing
page 23 | Laut & Leise: Art Director:
Jonas Natterer
pages 19, 22, 23, 108

POLLY VERITY
United Kingdom | www.polyscene.com
    page 108: Model: Carfax
    page 171: Photos by CS Stevens
pages 107, 108, 167, 171

POSTLERFERGUSON
United Kingdom | www.postlerferguson.com
pages 64, 65

PUBLIQUE LIVING
USA | www.publiqueliving.com
page 54

PUNGA
Argentina | www.punga.tv
    Tenmaiken spots; Production Company:
    PUNGA | Agency: La Comunidad |
    Client: Temaiken | Direction: Tomi Di |
    Executive Producer: Patricio Verdi |
    Art Direction: Tomi Di | Character
    Design: Gabriel Fermanelli | 3D Team
    Direction: Ruben Stremiz | Scenarios
    Design: Marilina Martignone
page 45 | VIDEO-DVD

RACHEL HOWE
USA | rachelhowe.blogspot.com
page 31

RICHARD SWEENEY
United Kingdom | www.richardsweeney.co.uk
pages 58, 106, 165, 167, 231

ROADSIDE PROJECTS
USA | www.roadsideprojects.com
page 41

ROBERT THE
USA | www.bookdust.com
    Images and pattern © 2008 Robert The
pages 150 - 152

RYUJI NAKAMURA
Japan | www.ryujinakamura.com
    Site: Prismic Gallery
pages 172, 173

SARAH ILLENBERGER
Germany | www.sarahillenberger.com
    page 51: Photo by Mathias Wehovsky
    page 52: Photos by Ragnar Schmuck
    page 176: Artwork and Photography:
    Sarah Illenberger
    pages 177-179: Photos by Ragnar
    Schmuck | Assistance: Katrin Rodegast
pages 51 - 52, 58, 176 - 179

SARAH KUENG & LOVIS CAPUTO
Switzerland | www.kueng-caputo.ch
    Producer: www.pensionfuerprodukte.de |
    Photo (upper image) by Raphael Hefti
page 53

SHAZ MADANI
United Kingdom | www.smadani.com
    pages 14, 42: In collaboration with
    Patrick Fry | www.patrickfry.co.uk
    page 243: Commissioned by: Ideas Factory
    | Client: Douglas and Gordon
pages 14, 42, 243

SHIN TANAKA
Japan | www.shin.co.nr
    page 85 | 4-in-1 robot: In collaboration
    with GIANT ROBOT & SCION
pages 84, 85 | DVD-ROM

SILJA GOETZ
Spain | www.siljagoetz.com
pages 37, 100, 101

SIMON ELVINS
United Kingdom | www.simonelvins.com
page 58

SIPHO MABONA / MABONA ORIGAMI
Switzerland | www.mabonaorigami.com
    Origami In the Pursuit of Perfection:
    Creative Director: Lars Ruehmann
    (Nordpol+ Hamburg) | Copy Writer:
    Sebastian Behrendt (Nordpol+ Hamburg)
    | Art Director: Sean Kirby (Nordpol+
    Hamburg) | Director: Tim Schierwater
    (Nordpol+ Hamburg) | Producer: Florian
    Liertz | Origami Artist: Sipho Mabona
    (Mabona Origami) | 3D Artists:
    André Junker & Christoffer Wolters
    (Nform) | Stoptrick Animation: Jim
    Lacy & Kathrin Albers (Stoptrick
    Hamburg) | Post Production: Acolori
    Medienproduktions GmbH | Sound
    Design: Audioforce Primetime Studios
page 193

SJORS TRIMBACH
Netherlands | www.sjorstrimbach.com
    page 74 | HF: www.hifructose.com
    page 87: In collaboration with
    Sergey Safonov
pages 68, 74, 87 | DVD-ROM

STEALTH.UNLIMITED
Netherlands | www.stealth.ultd.net
    Photos by STEALTH.unlimited;
    Featured Artists: Strange Attractors |
    www.strangeattractors.com;
    Cucosa artists collective | www.cucosa.nl;
    Robbert de Vrieze |
    www.gevondenontwerpen.nl
pages 236, 237

SUMER EREK
United Kingdom | www.sumererek.com
    Photos by Sumer Erek | Produced by
    Creative City.
pages 248, 249

SUSY OLIVEIRA
Canada | www.susyoliveira.ca
pages 182, 183

SWOON
USA | www.switchbacksea.org |
www.missrockaway.org
pages 215 - 218

TAYLOR MCKIMENS
USA | www.taylormckimens.com
page 207

THOMAS ALLEN
USA | www.thomasallenonline.com
    Courtesy of Foley Gallery (NY) and
    Thomas Barry Fine Arts (MN)
pages 185, 197

THORBJØRN ANKERSTJERNE & JONAS LUND
United Kingdom | www.ankerstjerne.co.uk |
www.jonaslund.co.uk
page 24

TITHI KUTCHAMUCH & NUTRE ARAYAVANISH
United Kingdom | www.tt-nt.info
    Photos by Suratchai C.
page 55

TOKUJIN YOSHIOKA
Japan | www.tokujin.com
page 240

TOYKYO
Belgium | www.toykyo.be
    pages 111, 208: Photos by Edelweiss studio
    pages 188, 205: Photos by Benjamin
    van Oost
pages 18, 111, 188, 205, 208

TUBBYPAWS
United Kingdom | www.tubbypaws.com
page 73 | DVD-ROM

YU JORDY FU
United Kingdom | www.jordyfu.com
pages 142, 143

YULIA BRODSKAYA
United Kingdom | www.artyulia.com
    pages 5-7: Photos by Michael Leznik
    page 7 | Darwin was wrong:
    Art director: Alison Lawn
    page 8: Art director: Richard Turley |
    Photo by David Levene
pages 5 - 8

# Templates

*PRINT | CUT | BUILD*

01   02 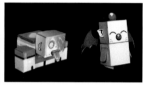 03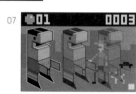

04  05

06     07

08   09  10

11  12  13

14    15  16

17    18

01 **MARSHALL ALEXANDER**
Bite Me
Foldskool Heroes series - 64KRAM
Foldskool Heroes series - Junior
Foldskool Heroes series - Nolan
Foldskool Heroes series - TRON Boy

02 **LOCOGRAFIX - PLAYROLL**
Crash Test Bunny

03 **KENN MUNK**
Antlor – SecuriTV

04 **SHIN TANAKA**
Hoophy 'We don't need Fake'

05 **JASON HARLAN**
Series Four - Tired of Death
Roboboxpunx
Series One - Boxwell Demon & Series Six - Mog
Series One - Schoolgirl

06 **HORRORWOOD**
Toro Oscuro
Ghosts in the Machine
Retro Demon
A Bad Dream on Birch Street

07 **PAPER FOLDABLES**
Edtari

08 **DIRK BEHLAU**
The Pixeleye Papertoy
In collaboration with Illunatic

09 **BRIAN GUBICZA**
E. A. Coobie (aka Paper Allan Poe)
Based on Wilfried Villain's 'Coobie'
Paper Toy template

10 **ANGELLO GARCÍA BASSI / CUBOTOY**
The God Eye
Marky

11 **ELOOLE**
Filomena

12 **SJORS TRIMBACH**
Speakerbooks

13 **MARK JAMES**
Snyrd
Based on a sketch by Pete Fowler
CardBoy
CardBoy Cartridges
Placid Casual - Chair

14 **IVAN RICCI**
Thai Ghost
Jagannatha
Based on Maarten Janssens
'BushDoctor' & '3eyedbear' template
Chicchirichì
Based on Josh McKibles 'NaniBird'
template

15 **TUBBYPAWS**
Little Street with Vending Machines

16 **NICOLA FROM BERN**
Foldschool - cardboard furniture

17 **CHRISTOPHER BONNETTE**
Squealer - Viking
Squealer - Krampus
Squealer - blank template
La Catrina Chibi Paper Toy

18 **FWIS**
Corbis Readymech Pinhole Camera - Peyote

*PLEASE REFER TO THE BOOK INDEX FOR CREDITS INFORMATION*

01

02

03

04

05

06

07

08

09

10

11

12

13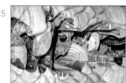

14

15

16

13

14

17

01 **APT & ASYLUM FILMS**
This is Where We Live

02 **1ST AVE MACHINE & PASSION PICTURES**
Audi Unboxed spot

03 **CARLO GIOVANI ESTÚDIO**
In collaboration with Lobo
Akatu Institute

04 **CARLO GIOVANI ESTÚDIO**
TIM Tales
Elma Chips Kids
Gordo Freak Show

05 **PUNGA**
Tenmaiken spots

06 **BENT IMAGE LAB**
Rob Shaw
They Might Be Giants 'I'm Impressed'

07 **ASIF MIAN/EVAQ**
Aesop Rock 'Fast Cars'

08 **BEN SCIASCIA**
Svelte 'Grind Your Bones'

09 **JULIEN VALLÉE & BLEUBLANCROUGE**
Black & White teaser

10 **GESTALTEN PODCAST WITH JULIEN VALLÉE**

11 **JESSE BROWN & SEAN PECKNOLD**
Fleet Foxes 'Mykonos'

12 **CIARA PHELAN**
Little Red

13 **JAVAN IVEY**
My Paper Mind

14 **GHOST ROBOT**
Bonnaroo Lineup Announcement 2009

15 **GESTALTEN PODCAST WITH BRIAN DETTMER**

16 **LOBO**
'Capitu' Opening Sequence
'Capitu' Title Cards
Making Of

17 **JEREMIAS BOETTCHER**
Papstars

*Design and Art with Paper*

Edited by Robert Klanten, Sven Ehmann and Birga Meyer
Text by Sonja Commentz
Preface by Robert Klanten

Layout by Birga Meyer for Gestalten
Typefaces: Generell TW by Mika Mischler, Naiv by Timo Gaessner
Foundry: www.gestalten.com/fonts
Cover typeface: Fisher by Atelier télescopique
Cover artwork by Sarah Illenberger, Photo by Ragnar Schmuck

Project management by Julian Sorge for Gestalten
Production management by Janine Milstrey for Gestalten
Production assistance by Natalie Reed for Gestalten
Special thanks to Ole Wagner
Proofreading by Patricia Goren
Printed SIA Livonia Print, Latvia

Published by Gestalten, Berlin
ISBN 978-3-89955-251-5
2nd printing 2010

© Die Gestalten Verlag GmbH & Co. KG, Berlin 2009
All rights reserved. No part of this publication may be reproduced
or transmitted in any form or by any means, electronic or mechanical,
including photocopy or any storage and retrieval system, without
permission in writing from the publisher.

Respect copyrights, encourage creativity!

For more information, please check www.gestalten.com

Bibliographic information published by the Deutsche Nationalbibliothek.
The Deutsche Nationalbibliothek lists this publication in the Deutsche
Nationalbibliografie; detailed bibliographic data is available on the
internet at http://dnb.d-nb.de.

None of the content in this book was published in exchange for payment
by commercial parties or designers; Gestalten selected all included work
based solely on its artistic merit.

This book was printed according to the internationally accepted FSC
standards for environmental protection, which specify requirements
for an environmental management system.

**Mixed Sources**
Product group from well-managed
forests and other controlled sources
www.fsc.org  Cert no. SW-COC-002883
© 1996 Forest Stewardship Council

Gestalten is a climate neutral company and so are our products.
We collaborate with the non-profit carbon offset provider myclimate
(www.myclimate.org) to neutralize the company's carbon footprint
produced through our worldwide business activities by investing in
projects that reduce $CO_2$ emissions (www.gestalten.com/myclimate).

Protect our planet

We hope you enjoy this book! While we hope it inspires you to work
with this multifaceted material, we hope it will equally inspire you to
reevaluate your relationship with paper. Paper is and will remain an
integral part of our daily life but there is a price to pay for our love
affair with paper. Therefore, it is important as a consumer to have
a clear understanding of the environmental issues surrounding the
manufacture of paper and make informed choices about the use of this
essential product. If you are considering using this invaluable material,
please use it wisely and be mindful of recycling – we certainly do.
Our combined efforts will help reduce the consumption of our precious
natural resources.

Leeds College of
LIBRARY
23·3·10
745.54
KLA
Art & Design

R 57012N

JEN STARK
How to Become a Millionaire
in 100 Days